Praise for
11 Principles of a Reagan Conservative

"A clear, concise outline of President Reagan's approach to politics—and a roadmap to victory for today's conservatives."

~ **Herb Meyer, Special Assistant to the Director of Central Intelligence and Vice Chairman of the CIA's National Intelligence Council during the Reagan Administration**

"Paul Kengor has done a great job and great service capturing the essence of Reagan's economic ideals. As someone involved with Reaganomics, and particularly tax cuts, I am especially pleased with Kengor's treatment of the subject. We need to properly understand what happened under Ronald Reagan in the 1980s—most notably, the enduring value of his tax cuts, which were a cornerstone of Reagan conservatism. This book gets it right. Nicely DONE."

~ **Dr. Arthur B. Laffer, the founder and chairman of Laffer Associates, an economic research firm**

"Paul Kengor has written an elegant primer on what Ronald Reagan believed, how he implemented so much of what he believed, and how it benefited the Republic. Here is essential reading for all who would vote for a better America."

~ **R. Emmett Tyrrell, Jr., founder and editor-in-chief of *The American Spectator***

"This succinct statement of the PRINCIPLES OF A REAGAN CONSERVATIVE, presented with a highly laudatory preface by Edwin Meese III, is sharp and well conceived. In this season, while we wait and pray for another Reagan, now in a time as dire as when Reagan took office amid domestic and foreign crises of the worst sort, this book will help us sort out the wheat from the chaff. It is not ideological purity that Reagan sought, but fidelity to practical, well-tested and proven principles. So many were against him, derisive and mocking. He smiled at them and continued in his quiet, courageous way, all the while careful never to violate the Eleventh Commandment: 'Speak ill of no other conservative—it takes all types.'"

~ **Michael Novak, 1994 Templeton Laureate**

"'What is a Reagan conservative?' That's a question that I, as a Reagan conservative and a Reagan biographer, get asked frequently. It's also a question that few self-described conservatives truly understand. And yet, with all the books on Ronald Reagan, this is the first to undertake an answer. Paul Kengor, himself a Reagan conservative, lays out 11 principles

of Reagan conservatism. This book couldn't be more timely and more needed as conservatives look desperately for the next generation of genuine Reagan conservatives."

~ Craig Shirley, Reagan biographer and
***New York Times* best-selling author**

"There are few historians who are closer students of the Reagan message, his thoughts, his utterances, and his convictions than Paul Kengor. In this primer of Reagan principles, Kengor offers us the heart of the Reagan vision."

~ Bill Bennett, former U.S. Secretary of Education
and host of "Morning in America"

"It's really a handy volume for the young people who won't read longer ones. Paul Kengor reminds us of the building blocks of successful modern conservatism. He adds and multiplies to bring us back together with Ronald Reagan's basic principles that are unifying for all of us. Paul Kengor reminds us of what ties us together. His discussion of Ronald Reagan's principles will inspire future generations to come together and promote a true conservative future. Kengor is a noted authority on Ronald Reagan. This slim volume distills the principles of Reagan for future generations to learn and apply for rebuilding a free society."

~ Ed Feulner, retired president of
The Heritage Foundation

"Few writers have studied and written about Ronald Reagan more comprehensively than Dr. Paul Kengor. None offers a clearer view of the personal compass (core beliefs) that guided Reagan the man, the conservative leader, and the most successful president in modern history. In 11 Principles of a Reagan Conservative, Kengor spells out the timeless tenets that made Reagan unique in his time, and that can also revive our spirit, enlighten and inspire our people, and restore our purpose to rebuild a strong America."

~Bently Elliott, former Director of White House Speechwriting
under President Reagan

"Ronald Reagan presents the rare combination of forward-looking with a back-to-basics foundation. No one captures Reagan's practice better than Paul Kengor, and his latest effort is an indispensable guide for everyone who wishes to extend the Reagan legacy for the next generation."

~Steven Hayward, author
The Age of Reagan

11 Principles of a Reagan Conservative

Paul Kengor

Beaufort Books
New York

ii - Paul Kengor

Library of Congress Cataloging-in-Publication Data

Kengor, Paul, 1966-
11 Principles of a Reagan Conservative / Paul Kengor, PhD.
— First edition.

Includes bibliographical references.
ISBN: 9780825308284 (pbk. : alk. paper)
1. Conservatism—United States. 2. Conservatism—United States—
Philosophy. 3. Reagan, Ronald—Influence. 4. United States—Politics and
government. I. Title. II. Title: Eleven Principles of a Reagan Conservative.
JC573.2.U6K46   2014
320.520973—dc23
2013036764

For inquiries about volume orders, please contact:

Beaufort Books
27 West 20th Street,
Suite 1102
New York, NY 10011
sales@beaufortbooks.com

Published in the United States by Beaufort Books
www.beaufortbooks.com

Distributed by Midpoint Trade Books
www.midpointtrade.com

Printed in the United States of America

Interior design by Vally Sharpe
Cover Design by Howard Grossman

Also by the Author

*All the Dupes Fit to Print: Journalists Who Have Served
as Tools of Communist Propaganda*

*The Communist: Frank Marshall Davis,
the Untold Story of Barack Obama's Mentor*

*Dupes: How America's Adversaries Have
Manipulated Progressives for a Century*

The Crusader: Ronald Reagan and the Fall of Communism

The Judge: William P. Clark, Ronald Reagan's Top Hand
(with Patricia Clark Doerner)

God and Ronald Reagan: A Spiritual Life

God and George W. Bush: A Spiritual Life

God and Hillary Clinton: A Spiritual Life

The Reagan Legacy: Assessing the Man and His Presidency
(with Peter Schweizer)

*Wreath Layer or Policy Player?
The Vice President's Role in Foreign Policy*

Contents

Foreword

By Edwin Meese III

When Ronald Reagan was inaugurated as president on January 20, 1981, he was immediately confronted by one of the most daunting combinations of challenges ever faced by a newly elected chief executive. On the domestic scene, the nation was gripped by the worst economic crisis since the Great Depression. Record high inflation and massive unemployment created a "misery index" of unprecedented proportions. An energy shortage and accelerating gasoline prices affected the well-being of families and businesses alike.

In terms of national security, the situation was equally bleak. In the aftermath of the Vietnam War, our military capability had eroded dramatically and the United States was too often regarded as neither a credible deterrent to our enemies nor a reliable ally to our friends. At the same time, the Soviet Union was adopting a more aggressive posture, endangering smaller governments throughout the world while it continued its cruel oppression of the captive nations behind the "Iron Curtain." Increasing world tensions and the threat of nuclear war were an ever-present menace.

At home, the dire economic conditions, the deteriorating international situation, and the seeming inability of the federal government to cope with a massive array of problems, had seriously affected the public's confidence in our nation and its institutions. The outgoing president had even proclaimed that the people were in a "malaise."

President Reagan responded with a new message, a new strategy, and a new direction for the nation. In this new, national forum he repeated a theme that he had championed as governor of California and in innumerable political speeches. He recalled the principles and values of our country's founders, which had been the foundation for America's success in the past. He promised to launch what he called a bold, forward-looking, conservative agenda, based on that foundation. He assured the nation, "I have seen the conservative future and it works."

Ronald Reagan did indeed change the nation. During his two terms as president, he revitalized the economy, he rebuilt our military capability, and he reinvigorated the spirit of the American people. He also changed the world, by working with other international leaders to set in motion the forces that led to the successful end of the Cold War—with the cause of freedom winning—and the ultimate implosion of the Soviet Union itself.

By these achievements and his successful leadership at home and abroad, Ronald Reagan completed the ascendency of conservatism as it developed from an intellectual and political exercise into a truly *governing* movement.

But a quarter of a century later, the questions, "What is 'Reagan conservatism?'" and "What does it mean for America today?" puzzle politicians and journalists. Historian Paul Kengor has set out to answer those questions in this book, *11 Principles of a Reagan Conservative*. Having written several books and numerous articles about Ronald Reagan, Kengor has brought extensive research and careful analysis to this examination of an intriguing political phenomenon, the importance of which endures.

Indeed, the questions and discussion of Reagan conservatism abound: How has conservatism remained vibrant despite massive opposition from most of the news media, much of academia, and the so-called "progressive" political establishment? How is it that Ronald Reagan was the president most talked about during the most recent presidential elections? Do the ideas that supported

Reagan's successful governance still pertain to today's problems? Professor Kengor opens his book with Reagan's own words about the meaning and significance of conservatism as he saw it:

The principles of conservatism are sound because they are based on what men and women have discovered through experience in not just one generation or a dozen, but in all the combined experience of mankind.

This book acknowledges, as did Reagan, that conservatism can "mean different things to those who call themselves conservatives." But, again by using Reagan's words, decisions, and actions, basic concepts of Reagan conservatism become clear through the president's consistency and clarity in the expression of his ideas. As the author summarizes, "The essence of conservatism is to preserve and conserve time-tested values that have endured for good reason and for the best of society, for citizens, for country, and for order ... " It is this collection of 11 clear principles that emerge from Ronald Reagan's own views that his basic philosophy of conservatism can be divined. As the author states, these specific beliefs, while not necessarily a comprehensive inventory, do provide definitive ideas that undergirded Reagan's thinking and actions as president and as a public figure.

The 11 principles that Professor Kengor uses to define a "Reagan conservative" are: Freedom, Faith, Family, Sanctity and Dignity of Human Life, American Exceptionalism, the Founders' Wisdom and Vision, Lower Taxes, Limited Government, Peace Through Strength, Anti-communism, and Belief in the Individual.

This book shows that, for the most part, these are not isolated concepts. The expression and implementation of any one idea is frequently related to one or more of the others. For example, the principle of freedom, which was key to much of Reagan's thinking, is derived from his extensive study of the founders' wisdom and vision, but is also extremely relevant to all of the other principles. The importance of being an American was the basis for American exceptionalism and our success in the world, and was the reason for limited government. To Reagan, lower taxes was not just a fiscal matter, but was also a freedom issue: You were more free if the government took less of your earnings, allowing you to decide how your money should be spent. Therefore, taxes should be only the amount needed to support the legitimate and necessary functions of a limited government.

Freedom, anti-communism, and peace through strength were all woven together into Reagan's thinking about national security. As Professor Kengor states, "Few things so typified Reagan quite like his stalwart anti-communism." He had experienced Marxism personally, as the Communist Party USA tried to take over the movie industry when Reagan was president of the Screen Actors Guild. He led several of the Hollywood unions to block the communist endeavor, despite enduring threats, intimidation, and violence. Throughout his professional life he studied communism in all its forms. As both a citizen and a public official, he led the fight against Marxism-Leninism, which he viewed as "the force of evil in the modern world" and "an absolute enemy of human freedom." The Reagan doctrine of Peace Through Strength and the major build-up of our military capability was a direct response to the threat of communism.

Although he was careful not to do anything that would cause someone to claim he was using his religion for political purposes, Ronald Reagan was a man of great faith. His personal belief in God and his devotion to Christian values animated his views on the importance of the family, on the sanctity and dignity of human life, and on the value and potential of the individual. It was also instrumental in his dedication to freedom. Like the founders, Reagan believed that the right to liberty was given by God and was a universal principle that conservatives have a duty to protect for the benefit of a greater humanity.

By numerous examples, Dr. Kengor demonstrates how the eleven basic principles, exercised in a cohesive way, enabled Reagan to show, both as governor and as president, that conservative ideas work. They also provided the opportunity for him to present the deeper message of conservatism to the American people. Beyond using these concepts as the basis for decision-making and executive actions, Reagan continually explained to his fellow citizens, as he liked to call them, how the principles of conservatism were essential to a successful democratic republic. In frequent messages from the Oval Office and in numerous speeches at public events, he emphasized how the values and precepts that had begun with the founders continued to be essential to opportunity, prosperity, and security for the nation. For Reagan, this political philosophy was not just a history lesson about the past but was a prescription for the nation's continued success in the future. This book describes his belief that our country was the very essence of a constitutional government and a representative republic.

Having had the privilege of serving with Ronald Reagan for over thirty years, and having the opportunity of firsthand observation of him as leader and teacher of the nation—indeed, in many ways, of the world—I can attest to his understanding of the power of conservative ideas and his integrity in using that power for the benefit of humanity, rather than personal or political gain.

Beyond the astute examination of Reagan's principles and the essence of his conservative philosophy, Dr. Kengor has done the reader a great service in presenting some of the president's most significant speeches. These remarks, delivered at critical times in our nation's history, illustrate the lessons that are such a valuable part of the Reagan legacy. Ranging from his preparation to govern to the culmination of his successful presidency, the president's own words are the enduring evidence of his sincerity, his humor, and his wisdom.

The late Dr. J. Rufus Fears, an esteemed historian who has written about leaders throughout the centuries, defined the difference between a politician and a statesman as the latter having four qualities: a bedrock of principles; a moral compass; a vision of where he sought to lead; and the ability to persuade and gain adherents to that vision.

Ronald Reagan had all of these attributes. This book recounts how he used his sound principles and remarkable personal capability to successfully lead a nation at a time of great challenge. And it provides a series of lessons about how conservative ideas can reward a wise people who are willing to adopt them today.

11 Principles of a Reagan Conservative

What Is a Reagan Conservative?

> The principles of conservatism are sound because they are based on what men and women have discovered through experience in not just one generation or a dozen, but in all the combined experience of mankind … I have seen the conservative future and it works … Our task now is not to sell a philosophy, but to make the majority of Americans, who already share that philosophy, see that modern conservatism offers them a political home.
>
> —*Ronald Reagan, February 6, 1977—*

What is a "Reagan conservative"? This is no minor question. At the time of the writing of this book, a Google search on the words "Reagan conservative" yields over thirty million results. And the question is hardly irrelevant to modern Republicans. Quite the contrary—it seems that every Republican presidential aspirant claims the mantle of Ronald Reagan.

That is not surprising. Politically speaking, Reagan was enormously successful. He won the presidency in 1980 by defeating an incumbent in a landslide, winning forty-four of fifty states, and then got reelected in 1984 by sweeping forty-nine of fifty states—including the most liberal among them, from California to Massachusetts, from the entirety of the West Coast to all of New England. He twice won blue states that Republicans today can only dream of winning. In these two elections, Reagan won the Electoral College by a combined margin of 1,014 to 62, and he did so when the majority of American voters were registered Democrats. Few presidents enjoyed such decisive success at the ballot box and in office generally. He left the White House with the highest public approval of any president since Eisenhower.

Reagan's presidential success is all the more notable when juxtaposed with the presidential careers of his contemporaries. Dating back to Lyndon B. Johnson, modern presidencies had ended in despair. LBJ, who replaced a president who was killed in office, was destroyed by Vietnam and decided not to pursue reelection. His successor, Richard Nixon, resigned in disgrace and suffered serious mental and physical repercussions. The office depressed and debilitated Nixon. His replacement, the uninspiring Gerald Ford, was unable to win a single election. Ford promptly lost to Jimmy Carter, whose own presidency was resoundingly rejected; to this day, one senses Carter's lingering feeling of rejection.

In the other direction, prior to Eisenhower, Harry Truman left office with an approval rating near 20 percent. He called the White House the "Great White Jail." Among other twentieth-century presidents, the job took its toll on Herbert Hoover, Warren Harding, Calvin Coolidge, and William Howard Taft; it ruined Woodrow Wilson, to the point of Wilson suffering several crushing strokes while he was president. Franklin Delano Roosevelt died in office.

After Reagan, George H. W. Bush, Reagan's vice president and White House successor, won only one term. He was defeated by Bill Clinton, who won two terms but never with more than 50 percent of the vote, and was impeached. Following Clinton was George W. Bush, who, though likewise winning two terms, had a very difficult presidency. A December 2006 Gallup poll found that Americans considered George W. Bush the most unsuccessful of modern presidents, with an approval rating even lower than Carter and Nixon. Bush registered the highest disapproval of any president since Truman.

And though Barack Obama won two terms, he was the first president in history to be reelected with fewer popular and Electoral College votes than he received in 2008. Obama won a bare majority of states in 2012—only twenty-six of them. And should we even mention counties? The county map under Reagan was a sea of red, and it remained a sea of red still under Obama.

Unlike so many presidents, Ronald Reagan made the job look easy. In fact, Reagan's stock has only risen, continuing well beyond his tenure in the Oval Office. In that same December 2006 Gallup poll that revealed George W. Bush's unpopularity, 64 percent of respondents judged Reagan an outstanding or above-average president and only 10 percent rated him below average or poor. Each year, Gallup releases its annual poll for Presidents' Day, asking Americans to judge the "greatest president" of all time. Gallup began asking the "greatest president" question in 1999. Of the thirteen times Gallup has done the survey, the public placed Reagan first four times—2001, 2005, 2011, and 2012—and always in the top three. Reagan typically beats Lincoln.

Many such polls could be cited. A Zogby poll released for Presidents' Day 2011—the centennial of Reagan's birth—which asked the public to rate presidents since World War II, listed Reagan as the "greatest," with FDR second and Kennedy third.[1]

Even then, Reagan's support transcends the presidency. An extraordinary June 2005 online poll by the Discovery Channel and AOL (which included 2.4 million responses) declared Reagan the "greatest American of all time," beating Lincoln and Washington.[2]

Reagan also beats Barack Obama. A poll conducted shortly after Obama's second inaugural asked Americans who they would vote for in a presidential contest between Reagan and Obama. Reagan won in a landslide, taking 58 percent of the vote, an even higher total than his trouncing of Jimmy Carter in 1980. Remarkably, Reagan even defeated Obama among voters aged eighteen to thirty-four, the powerful youth segment that swept Obama into the White House.[3]

In sum, all of this is one way of helping to explain why Ronald Reagan has become the gold standard for Republican presidential nominees. What Republican would not aspire to this kind of public approval?

But not only would Republican presidential aspirants like to emulate Reagan's political appeal; they are also quick to identify with his brand of conservatism. As Republican candidates every four years jockey for their party's presidential nomination, they invoke Ronald Reagan: "I believe as Ronald Reagan believed ..."

What Did Reagan Believe?

This begs the paramount question of what Ronald Reagan believed. As a Reagan biographer, the questions I'm most frequently asked by Republican voters and pundits and media types of all stripes go something like this: *What would Reagan do if he were president right now? Where would Reagan stand on this issue? Which candidate is most like Reagan? Who's the next Ronald Reagan? What did Ronald Reagan really believe?*

Such questions can be difficult to answer, and the answers often would surprise many of those begging a response. For example, would Reagan have endorsed George W. Bush's attempt to expand Reagan's "March of Freedom" from the former Soviet empire into the Middle East? Bush, after all, invoked precisely that "March" as a chief motivation for his Middle East policies and actions.[4] Would Reagan have raised the debt ceiling during the bitter debate between President Obama and the Republican Congress in the summer of 2012? All sorts of media sources, especially on the liberal side, insisted he would have done so. Would Reagan have acquiesced to an increase in income taxes in 2013? Here again, liberals assured us he would. What was Reagan's position on immigration? I'm always taken aback by certain voices on the right invoking the name of Reagan as they demand immediate deportation of all illegal immigrants.

Conservatives and liberals alike might be surprised by the answers to some of these questions.

And how did Reagan himself see conservatism? Speaking in October 1983 to the house of conservatism, the Heritage Foundation, Reagan quipped, "During the years when I was out on the mashed-potatoes circuit [i.e., a popular dinner speaker] I was sometimes asked to define conservatism, and I must confess that, while I have the cream of the conservative intellectual movement before me, I'm tempted to use Justice Potter Stewart's definition. He gave it for another subject, by the way. He said he couldn't define it exactly, but 'I know it when I see it.'"[5]

Fair enough. We can take Reagan at his word that he understood conservatism when he saw it. But do *we* know it when we see it? Many professing conservatives think they know it when they see it, but clearly they don't all see eye to eye on a common definition. They do, however, tend to agree on one thing: When they see Ronald Reagan, they see conservatism. Reagan is synonymous with conservatism. Look up *conservatism* in a dictionary and you might just as well see a picture of Ronald Reagan.

Reagan's most frequent ruminations on conservatism came at CPAC, the Conservative Political Action Conference—an annual mecca of conservatives, where the disciples of Reagan and the likes of Buckley and Goldwater and Russell Kirk do pilgrimage. Reagan began speaking at CPAC in 1974, its first gathering. He addressed the faithful no less than thirteen times through his final year in the White House, not missing a single CPAC during any year of his presidency.[6] Perhaps his most vigorous defense of conservative thinking came in his 1977 CPAC remarks, delivered February 6, 1977—his sixty-sixth birthday.

There, Reagan began by conceding that conservatism can "mean different things to those who call themselves conservatives." He delineated positions that tend to identify social and economic conservatives. Reagan, for the record, was both a social and economic conservative; indeed, how could a *complete* conservative—which is really what Reagan was—be strictly one or the other?

The essence of conservatism is to preserve and conserve time-tested values that have endured for good reason and for the best of society, for citizens, for country, and for order—a brief summation that the late Russell Kirk, probably conservatism's preeminent philosophical spokesman, would have endorsed.[7] Conservatives aim to conserve. Ronald Reagan said much the same in this February 1977 speech:

> The common sense and common decency of ordinary men and women, working out their own lives in their own way—this is the heart of American conservatism today. Conservative wisdom and principles are derived from willingness to learn, not just from what is going on now, but from what has happened before.

> The principles of conservatism are sound because they are based on what men and women have discovered through experience in not just one generation or a dozen, but in all the combined experience of mankind. When we conservatives say that we know something about political affairs, and that we know can be stated as principles, we are saying that the principles we hold dear are those that have been found, through experience, to be ultimately beneficial for individuals, for families, for communities and for nations—found through the often bitter testing of pain or sacrifice and sorrow.[8]

Reagan then enunciated a number of conservative principles: freedom and liberty, free markets, religious freedom, constitutional rights and protections, anti-communism, smaller government, local government, individualism, voluntarism, communities, families, self-reliance, hard work, common sense, reason, faith in God. He called for a just and prudent government that spends money wisely and whose stewards act with integrity and honesty.

Reagan told the CPAC brethren that he believed the "old lines" once dividing social and economic conservatives were "disappearing." He hoped the time had come "to present a program of action based on political principle that can attract those interested in the so-called 'social' issues and those interested in 'economic' issues." Reagan asked, "In short, isn't it possible to combine the two major segments of contemporary American conservatism into one politically effective whole?"

Here was a form of what William F. Buckley Jr. and Frank Meyer, another influential conservative, had earlier called "fusionism."[9] Buckley's publication, *National Review*, the flagship of conservatism and a favorite of Reagan's, intended precisely that objective. Both Buckley and Reagan saw the conservative tent as wide enough for both social and economic conservatives. Neither should bar the other; both belonged—they were siblings.

That was what Reagan proposed in this particular CPAC speech, delivered not even a full year since his attempt to wrench the Republican Party nomination from the incumbent, President Gerald Ford—who Reagan rightly saw as not a conservative. At this point, Reagan was already positioning himself for a run in 1980 against the Democrat who defeated Ford, President Jimmy Carter. Reagan insisted that a "conservative majority" could emerge from within the fractured Republican Party to win back the White House and take America in a genuinely conservative direction.

"We can do it in America," Reagan assured. "This is not a dream, a wistful hope. It is and has been a reality. I have seen the conservative future and it works."

Reagan articulated a message that ought to resound with conservatives today: "Our task now is not to sell a philosophy, but to make the majority of Americans, who already share that philosophy, see that modern conservatism offers them a political home. We are not a cult, we are members of a majority. Let's act and talk like it." (Still today, Americans self-identify as conservative over liberal by a margin of almost two to one.[10])

This would require, said Reagan, an adherence to "political principle" and to "principled politics."

And after adhering to just that in his 1980 presidential campaign, thereby winning the presidency in a landslide, and getting reelected with that same philosophy and platform in 1984, Reagan would remain just as positive about the potency of a principled conservative message.

In February 1987, well into his second term after cruising back to the White House with the backing of every state in the nation but Minnesota (the home state of his Democrat challenger), Reagan told CPAC that the conservative movement remained in ascendancy because it had a "bold, forward-looking agenda."[11]

In his final presidential address to CPAC in February 1988, Reagan said that conservatives must always "vote for limited government, family values, and a tough, strong foreign policy." Reagan said that conservatives should vote for such a platform unfailingly, "every single time." Such conservatives are "believers in common sense and sound values."[12]

Yet, even with these Reagan ruminations on conservatism, developing a single, succinct definition can be elusive. It is often easier to define conservatism not in general philosophical terms but according to certain principles and clear policy positions. That is also true for Reagan conservatism. Reagan, in fact, did a masterful job of coalescing conservatism (and conservatives and their country) around certain key principles and policies and issues. He viewed conservatism as a practical ideology given to practical application. Reagan told CPAC that conservatism was one political viewpoint mercifully "free from slavish adherence to abstraction."[13]

For Reagan, conservatism was a principled ideology from which cohesive principles emerged.

11 Principles of Reagan Conservatism

And so, easier than philosophical abstraction is delineating certain core Reagan principles—the underlying thinking that formed the basis of Reagan's political philosophy and even political behavior. These principles not only rallied conservatives but also helped unite a wider electorate and fuel the Reagan revolution.

Thus, we arrive at the heart of this book: what I call my "Reagan Eleven"; that is, 11 specific beliefs that undergirded Reagan's thinking and actions as president and as a public figure.[14] The list is not the be-all-and-end-all; it is not a comprehensive inventory that magically encompasses the entirety of Ronald Reagan's thinking. It does, however, get us closer to the crux of what Reagan's conservatism was about and what his emulators today might take to heart.

Here are those 11 principles of Reagan conservatism:

- **Freedom**
- **Faith**
- **Family**
- **Sanctity and dignity of human life**
- **American exceptionalism**
- **The Founders' wisdom and vision**
- **Lower taxes**
- **Limited government**
- **Peace through strength**
- **Anti-communism**
- **Belief in the individual**

Here, I will offer a somewhat brief examination of each of these 11 and what they meant to Ronald Reagan and his brand of conservatism. The categories are not airtight and often overlap—as perhaps they should, given that they derive from and also form an integrated, cohesive philosophy. Taken together, they provide contours in defining and explaining what we frequently but often too casually refer to as "Reagan conservatism."

Freedom

Ronald Reagan spoke constantly of freedom. Mankind, from "the swamps to the stars," as he noted in his seminal October 1964 "Time for Choosing" speech, longed to be free. The global Cold War struggle of Reagan's life represented the arc of that longing, of that crisis. As president, Reagan happily assumed the role of freedom's voice to the "captive peoples" in the "captive nations" languishing behind the Iron Curtain.

By Reagan's reckoning, all people everywhere, without exception, needed to know freedom. Obviously, the communist world hungered for it. But even the free world didn't always appreciate it. Free people needed always to be reminded of their freedom and the need to understand and reassert it. That included Americans.

In his swan song to the American people, his moving Farewell Address, January 11, 1989, Reagan spoke almost mystically, poetically of "freedom man." He told a story, as he was good at doing, one that harkened back to a story he had shared in the "Time for Choosing" speech that first launched him onto the national political stage. Back then, it was the story of a Cuban refugee who escaped by boat. This time, it was the story of a Vietnamese refugee, one of the millions of boat people who escaped after Vietnam went communist. The president talked of staring out the White House window, increasingly pensive as his final days in the Oval Office waned:

I've been thinking a bit at that window. I've been reflecting on what the past eight years have meant and mean. And the image that comes to mind like a refrain is a nautical one—a small story about a big ship, and a refugee, and a sailor. It was back in the early '80s, at the height of the boat people. And the sailor was hard at work on the carrier *Midway*, which was patrolling the South China Sea. The sailor, like most American servicemen, was young, smart, and fiercely observant. The crew spied on the horizon a leaky little boat. And crammed inside were refugees from Indochina hoping to get to America. The *Midway* sent a small launch to bring them to the ship and safety. As the refugees made their way through the choppy seas, one spied the sailor on deck, and stood up, and called out to him. He yelled, "Hello, American sailor. Hello, freedom man."

Hello, American sailor. Hello, freedom man. This boat person, in the hands of Ronald Reagan, was not only a boat person but a spokesperson. He was a spokesperson like Reagan, testifying to a great America, to America as a beacon, to America as a bastion of freedom. He was an image and symbol of something that ran deeper than the South China Sea.

Reagan completed the thought on the boat person and on the sailor—that is, the American *freedom man*: "A small moment with a big meaning, a moment the sailor, who wrote it in a letter, couldn't get out of his mind. And, when I saw it, neither could I. Because that's what it was to be an American in the 1980s. We stood, again, for freedom."

That was quite a revealing statement. According to Ronald Reagan, to be an American in the 1980s—his era, his time, his presidency, his time for choosing—was to stand for one thing in particular: freedom.

And for Reagan, to be a conservative was to stand for freedom.

Freedom had many manifestations in Reagan's mind. It related (as we will see later) to taxes and regulations. The more the government takes in taxes, the less freedom the individual has with money earned. If the government increases your taxes by 50 percent, you lose that much more money—money that might have been used to reduce a mortgage, pay off student loans, purchase a car, buy groceries, do home repairs, fix a broken dishwasher, hire a plumber or electrician, replace a lawn mower or do landscaping, or give to charity. When government takes that money, you lose the freedom to use that money. As for regulations, excessive regulations hinder or even halt the ability to open or operate a business, which, incidentally, provides jobs for others. The freedom to school your children as you please is another important freedom we enjoy in America. Freedom is indispensable to education not only from K–12 but also in higher education, as Reagan acutely understood.[15] Of course, there are the First Amendment freedoms: religion, speech, press, assembly. There is the freedom even to leave—to travel, to emigrate.

Reagan knew that freedom was the engine of American individualism and prosperity. He trusted individual Americans. He said the key was to "trust the people" and what they could do with their freedom: "Only when people are free to worship, create, and build, only when they can decide their destiny and benefit from their own risks—only then do societies become dynamic, prosperous."[16]

As an example, Reagan pointed to oil, stating that oil "was worthless until entrepreneurs with ideas and the freedom and faith to take risks managed to locate it, extract it, and put it to work for humanity." Indeed, added Reagan, Americans could "find more oil and we can develop abundant supplies of new forms of energy if we encourage risk-taking by thousands and thousands of entrepreneurs"—a lesson applicable today, as America's current White House leadership refuses to extract the vast reservoirs of oil under its own feet. The solution was to rely on American individuals rather than relying "on government to horde, ration, and control.

The whole idea is to trust the people."[17] Government needed to get out of the way.[18]

Reagan argued that "ingenuity, imagination, and creativity" are "the forces unleashed by human freedom." It was these forces, he said, that built America. If given the chance, these forces could "reshape the face of this planet." "It's only when people are free," said the president—whether "free to dream and discuss untried ideas" or "free in the marketplace"—that "innovation and opportunity can become the order of the day."[19] As "free men and women," there is "nothing we Americans cannot achieve."[20]

Here we see a common theme across and at the apex of Reagan's principles: his unwavering belief in the capabilities of the American people. These were capabilities fueled in large part by the force of freedom.

Significantly, this freedom principle was not just an American principle; for Reagan, it was a universal principle. Freedom was not the exclusive domain of Americans. Reagan said that freedom was "one of the deepest and noblest aspirations of the human spirit." All humans aspire for freedom. And when governments permit people to express their aspiration for freedom, especially in the economic sphere, freedom works. Reagan told the United Nations flatly, "the free market . . . works."[21]

Conservatives thus needed to be freedom fighters. According to Reagan, conservatives should not be simply anti–big government or anti-communist or against high taxes and burdensome regulations, but, in the positive, "keepers of the flame of liberty."[22] By Reagan's recounting, a conservative conserved freedom.

As such, this presented to conservatives a greater duty to greater humanity. For freedom men and women, it translated into a freedom role abroad—like that sailor bringing the boat person to freedom. Reagan told CPAC that conservatives believed that America "should be a source of support, both moral and material, for all those on God's Earth who struggle for freedom. Our cause is their cause."[23]

To be sure, this was not merely an abstract observation; this was a major foreign-policy pronouncement by the president. He highlighted the causes of those in Nicaragua, in Afghanistan, in Poland, and in Angola—all battling for freedom against communism. Said Reagan, "American foreign policy is not simply focused on the prevention of war but the expansion of freedom." As Reagan pushed to crush global communism, he also pushed for a "forward strategy for freedom," for a "march of freedom and democracy which will leave Marxism-Leninism on the ash heap of history as it has left other tyrannies which stifle the freedom and muzzle the self-expression of the people."[24]

But freedom had a core more dense and meaningful. Yes, it was at the crux of the epic battle of Reagan's time, the battle against totalitarian communism. But it was also at the crux of the battle against *atheistic* communism. Thus, there was something deeper still to this freedom thing.

As Reagan said in an October 1982 speech on communist-controlled Poland, a nation of repressed people that he saw as holding the potential to crack the entire Soviet Communist Bloc, "The struggle in the world today for the hearts and minds of mankind is based on one simple question: Is man born to be free, or slave? In country after country, people have long known the answer to that question. We are free by divine right."[25] Yes, a divine right to freedom—God-ordained. There is, said Reagan, a spiritual center at the "heart of freedom." It is there because each of us is made in the image of God "the Creator." It is this that is truly "our power" and "our freedom."[26] Honoring freedom was thus "redeeming" in the eyes of God.[27]

The Creator had created freedom. He had created man. He had created us to be free. Honoring freedom meant honoring the Creator and our divine right.

And Reagan knew that the disciples of "communist man" (i.e., the Soviet leadership) feared the "infectiousness" of freedom, especially its infectiousness within Communist Bloc countries.[28]

Reagan argued that the Soviet elite held power so tightly because, "as we have seen in Poland," they "fear what might happen if even the smallest amount of control slips from their grasp. They fear the infectiousness of even a little freedom."[29] Uncorking the "genie of freedom" could unravel the entire Soviet empire. It did just that, unraveling in 1989, the final year of Reagan's presidency.

When the Cold War was over, Reagan, no longer president, gave a speech in Cambridge, England, where he remarked on what Mikhail Gorbachev's taste of freedom had set loose, and set loose to Gorbachev's surprise. As for Reagan, he was not surprised at all: "As is always the case, once people who have been deprived of basic freedom taste a little of it, they want all of it. It was as if Gorbachev had uncorked a magic bottle and a genie floated out, never to be put back in again."[30]

You cannot deprive a people—any people—of their longing and right for basic freedom. It is a universal aspiration. Conservatives profess and fight for freedom. Reagan conservatism professes and fights for freedom.

Faith

Consistent with Reagan, conservatives today constantly talk of freedom. *Freedom. Freedom. Freedom.* Go to any gathering of conservatives, and you will hear a freedom mantra. They speak of "freedom" almost as if it were a one-word synonym for conservatism, a slogan for the movement. At times, they do so in an almost trite way, or at least so often that it almost seems trite. Reagan said that freedom is always under assault; every generation must fight to preserve it. Well, every generation also needs to clarify it, to teach it to the next.

Yet, in truth, as Reagan understood, to invoke freedom alone is a mistake. Freedom by itself, isolated, is libertarianism, not conservatism. For the conservative, freedom requires faith; it should never be decoupled from faith. Freedom not rooted in faith can lead to moral anarchy, which, in turn, creates social and cultural chaos. Freedom without faith is the Las Vegas Strip, not the City of God. Freedom without faith begets license and invites vice rather than virtue. Faith infuses the soul with a sanctifying grace that allows humans in a free society to love and serve their neighbors, to think about more than themselves. We aspire to our better angels when our faith nurtures and elevates our free will.

Genuine freedom—and certainly the Christian conception of freedom—is not license. To a practicing Christian, freedom cannot be practiced without faith. As noted by Pope John Paul II, with whom Reagan had an excellent relationship of strong mutual respect and collaboration,[31] without the rock and rudder of faith, freedom can become confused, perverse, and can even lead to the destruction of freedom for others.[32] John Paul II's successor, Pope Benedict XVI, said that the West suffers from a "confused ideology of freedom," one that has unleashed a modern "dictatorship of relativism."[33]

In the New Testament, Galatians 5:13-14 states, "For you were called for freedom, brothers. But do not use your freedom as opportunities for the flesh; rather, serve one another through love. For the whole law is fulfilled in one statement, namely, 'You shall love your neighbor as yourself.'"

The great conservative thinker Russell Kirk, in his 1974 classic *The Roots of American Order*, spoke of "ordered liberty." Kirk talked of the need for "inner order" by American citizens before they and their countrymen and country could successfully govern through "outer order." Ordering ourselves *internally* was critical to the nation's *external* order. The nation's first president, George Washington, argued the same, stressing the need for citizens to self-govern themselves before they could self-govern their nation.

Ronald Reagan believed this wholeheartedly.[34] He felt that God provided the route to goodness and wisdom; only through reliance in Divine Providence could America's leaders achieve goodness and wisdom. One of Reagan's favorite images was that of George Washington kneeling in the snow in prayer at Valley

Forge, which Reagan called the "most sublime image in American history."[35] Washington kneeling in prayer, said Reagan in a radio address in December 1983, "personified a people who knew it was not enough to depend on their own courage and goodness; they must also seek help from God, their Father and their Preserver."[36]

It was God, Reagan maintained, "from whom all knowledge springs."[37] "When we open ourselves to Him," Reagan told a group of public-school students, "we gain not only moral courage but also intellectual strength."[38] The light of faith enlightens the intellect and our reason. Reagan had expressed this sentiment for years, long before the presidency.[39]

Such a divine source, Reagan reasoned, ought to be tapped.

Quite the contrary, Reagan was earnestly afraid of what happens to free, democratic societies when they scrap religious faith. To that end, one of Reagan's best speeches, and arguably one of the most forgotten, was an October 1988 address marking the bicentennial of Georgetown University. "At its full flowering, freedom is the first principle of society; this society, Western society," Reagan told students at Georgetown. "And yet freedom cannot exist alone. And that's why the theme for your bicentennial is so very apt: learning, faith, and freedom. Each reinforces the others, each makes the others possible. For what are they without each other?"

He asked his audience to pray that America be guided by learning, faith, and freedom. He quoted Alexis de Tocqueville, author of the nineteenth-century classic *Democracy in America*: "Tocqueville said it in 1835, and it's as true today as it was then: 'Despotism may govern without faith, but liberty cannot. Religion is more needed in democratic societies than in any other.'" With a nod to his academic audience, Reagan warned, "Learning is a good thing, but unless it's tempered by faith and a love of freedom, it can be very dangerous indeed. The names of many intellectuals are recorded on the rolls of infamy, from Robespierre to Lenin to Ho Chi Minh to Pol Pot."[40]

Reagan contended that one thing that "must never change" for America is that men and women must "seek Divine guidance in the policies of their government and the promulgation of their laws." They must, he urged, "make our laws and government not only a model to mankind, but a testament to the wisdom and mercy of God."[41]

Conservatives today quote a particular Reagan remark on freedom: "Freedom is never more than a generation from extinction … It must be fought for, protected, and handed on." So popular is this Reagan quotation that I own a coffee mug from a conservative organization with those words etched into the ceramic. Yes, Reagan said those words, and agreed with them, but Reagan did not want those generations fighting that fight without the shepherd of faith. Despots might attempt to govern without faith, but Americans should not. Faith and freedom reinforce one another, each making the other possible.

Reagan felt that *learning* was about learning this crucial relationship. It is telling that many of these Reagan remarks on the bond between faith and freedom were shared with students—that is, with those engaged in the process of learning. So, too, learning about and understanding conservatism—especially Reagan conservatism—is about knowing this reinforcing relationship.

More, learning about and understanding *America*, too, was about knowing this relationship. It is the "twin beacons of faith and freedom," proclaimed Reagan, that have "brightened the American sky."[42]

So, yes, faith and freedom are the bedrock of conservatism. They were the rudder that navigated Reagan through the tumult of his times and should likewise guide conservatives today.

Can one be a conservative without being religious? Russell Kirk observed that while not all religious people are conservatives, not all conservatives are religious people. "All the same," said Kirk, "there could be no conservatism without a religious foundation, and it is conservative people, by and large, who defend religion in our time."[43] Kirk said that over fifty years ago, and it's even truer today. A similar take was offered by William F. Buckley Jr., who observed that "a real conservative need not be religious but could not be hostile to religion."[44] At the least, that is true. Conservatism comes far easier to the religiously minded than the secularly inclined.

Ronald Reagan probably would have endorsed these observations.

But while the link between faith and freedom could and should typify any number of conservative thinkers, and certainly conservatism, there is another aspect of Reagan conservatism that was totally unique to Ronald Reagan. It is something that not every conservative shares: Reagan's unshakable faith-based optimism.

This was traceable to Reagan's upbringing, specifically to his mother Nelle.[45] His mother always insisted, under the worst of trials, that "God has a plan for all of us," one that in the end "always works out for the best." There are always life's "twists in the road," but there is also always a loving, all-wise God in control, who works everything according to His plans.[46]

Long before his presidency, as a thirty-nine-year-old movie star in Hollywood, Reagan in June 1950 published an article called "My Faith" in a Hollywood magazine. He finished the piece with a two-verse quote from a poem: "God's in His Heaven/All's right with the world." That conclusion, thirty years before his election as president, encapsulated his lifelong faith-based optimism.[47] Indeed, Reagan spoke of "God-given optimism."[48] His optimism, he said, came "from my strong faith in God," a blessing for which he was grateful to Divine Providence.[49]

A touching indication of this was a letter that Reagan, as governor, wrote to a New York woman about her handicapped son:

> I find myself believing very deeply that God has a plan for
> each one of us. Some with little faith and even less testing
> seem to miss in their mission, or else we perhaps fail to
> see their imprint on the lives of others. But bearing what

we cannot change and going on with what God has given us, confident there is a destiny, somehow seems to bring a reward we wouldn't exchange for any other. It takes a lot of fire and heat to make a piece of steel.[50]

Addressing her son directly, Reagan added that "things have a way of working out in life, and usually for the best, if we simply go forward doing our best and trusting that God does have a plan."[51] Even a disadvantaged situation might be part of the divine plan— or, as Reagan and his close friend and aide, Bill Clark, together called it, "the DP."[52] Things often work for the better, even if they look bleak in the short term.

In another letter he wrote as governor, Reagan told the widow of a slain policeman that no one can be sure of "the why of God's plan for us ... Whatever God's plan is for each of us, we can only trust in His wisdom and mercy ... It isn't given to us to understand—we can only have faith ... [W]e must have faith in God's plan for all of us."[53]

These are just a few of the innumerable letters Reagan sent all over the country to everyday people, preaching the gospel of "God's plan," the divine plan, the DP. It was a most optimistic vision.

Finally, another telling indication of Reagan's optimism was a favorite parable of his, an amusing anecdote about the pony in the dung heap.[54] It was a story about a father with two boys: a pessimist and an optimist. The father placed the pessimist in a room full of new toys. He placed the optimist in a barn with a pile of manure. When the father returned, the pessimist was crying and throwing a fit, complaining that he had no toys to play with. When he went to the barn, he found the optimist digging doggedly through the pile of manure. When the father asked the optimist what he was doing, the boy replied, "I know there's a pony in here somewhere!"

That optimist was Reagan. The kid in the manure was Ronald Reagan. This was a parable about himself.

And that optimism translated into so much of what he did as president, in foreign policy and domestic. As to the former, Reagan alone possessed a truly remarkable, self-assured certainty that he could win the Cold War when no one else anywhere put stock in the possibility, and amid naysayers all around him. He was confident America could win, and that he could play the role of rescuer in the intense Cold War drama—rescuing the world from the evils of atheistic Soviet communism. In January 1977, only days after Jimmy Carter had been inaugurated president, and when it looked like America was losing the Cold War, Regan told Richard V. Allen, a friend and foreign-policy adviser, "Dick, my idea of American policy toward the Soviet Union is simple, and some would say simplistic. It is this: We win and they lose. What do you think of that?"[55]

Most observers thought that crazy—impossible. Not Reagan. He was the world's leading optimist in an otherwise extremely pessimistic, dire international situation.

That was likewise true in domestic policy. As one Reagan adviser told *Time* magazine during the lingering recession of 1982–1983, when the stimulative effect of Reagan's tax cuts seemed slow in sparking the economy, "He is absolutely convinced that there will be a big recovery ... He is an optimist. My God is he an optimist!"[56]

The aide had unexpectedly touched upon Reagan's source for that optimism: God.

Reagan himself acknowledged that this optimism uniquely defined him. In a speech at the end of his presidency, he expressed it colorfully: "I know it's often said of me that I'm an optimist. Over the years, I've been described as an inveterate optimist, an eternal optimist, a reflexive optimist—a born optimist, a canny optimist, a cagey optimist—even as defiantly optimistic. It just goes to show there's no word that cannot be turned into a pejorative if the pundits work hard enough at it."[57]

Only Reagan himself could best express his optimism. He said it and showed it unlike anyone. And it was another way that faith so fundamentally affected his outlook, his life, his presidency, and his conservatism.

Family

The very Trinity that Ronald Reagan worshipped—Father, Son, and Holy Spirit—is a family, one that is foundational to human civilization. Perhaps it is no coincidence, then, that the family is the foundation of human civilization. The next generation cannot exist without the union of a man and a woman. Families not only produce the next generation, but good families and good parenting produce the next generation of good citizens.

Ronald Reagan's own family life had its share of issues, as does any family. His first marriage (to actress Jane Wyman) ended in a painful divorce he did not want and which he always regretted as a great personal failure. That marriage produced daughter Maureen; an adopted son, Michael;[58] and a daughter (Christine), who died shortly after a premature birth. Reagan's second marriage, to Nancy Davis, lasted the remainder of his many years, and was a lifelong romance of dedicated mutual commitment. It produced two children, Patti and Ron, whose occasional rocky relationship with their parents garnered headlines and controversy—some of which was embarrassing and politically charged—but was never without affection or reconciliation.[59]

As for his own upbringing, Reagan's family was not without challenges. His father lacked the devoutness and discipline of his mother, whereas his mother lacked the dreams and idealism of his father. The father, Jack Reagan, was the hopeless dreamer, while the mother, Nelle Reagan, was the hopeful prayer. Between Jack's dreaming and Nelle's grounding, Ronald secured reliable roots. He acquired unique skills and intangibles from both parents: Jack's gift of gab, storytelling, and idealism; Nelle's dedication, forgiveness, perseverance, and cheerful piety. Nelle held the family together, suffering Jack's sins and struggles with heroic charity, a model of virtue that Reagan admired and remembered. From both parents, the young Reagan learned ethnic and religious and racial tolerance. He acquired lots of love from both of them. Any observer of Reagan's upbringing would describe it as hard, never knowing where the next dollar (or roof) might come from, but Reagan saw it as anything but. The born optimist described his childhood as idyllic, a Norman Rockwell portrait. He was nothing but grateful to his parents and the life they gave him. They were foundational.

As an adult and as president, Reagan returned the favor, extolling the family as "the most basic unity of society," as "the most important unit in society," as "the most durable of all institutions," as "the nucleus of civilization," "the cornerstone of American society," as the "engine of social progress." Families "stand at the center of society" and as the very "foundation of freedom." And children, said Reagan, "belong in a family."[60]

It is in a family that children are not only cared for but, said Reagan, "taught the moral values and traditions that give order and stability to our lives and to society as a whole." It was "more important than ever" that America's families "affirm an older and more lasting set of values."[61] In a decidedly conservative sentiment, Reagan insisted that it is up to families to "preserve and pass on to each succeeding generation the values we share and cherish."[62] In a likewise conservative sentiment, Reagan insisted that our "concept of the family" "must withstand the trends of lifestyle and legislation."[63] And concepts like fatherhood, said Reagan, should mean today what they have always meant in America.[64]

Those last sentences merit close inspection: Families preserve and conserve the time-tested values worth preserving and conserving. They do this among and across continuing generations. They must persevere in doing so against the often unhealthy onslaught of new trends and fads and fashions and legislation. Not every new change or new law is right, nor is (said Reagan) every fad or fashion.[65] "Progress" does not always progress toward the good (quite the contrary), especially when it latches on to the latest cultural dictate or fancy. The family, which is always older than the newest law or license, is a bulwark against the prevailing zeitgeist or latest cultural twaddle about "*lifestyle*."

Reagan's concept of the family was anchored by a loving mom and loving dad in a committed marital relationship. In one of the final formal proclamations issued during his presidency (January 12, 1989), Reagan insisted that "we must teach youngsters the beauty of the loving, lifelong relationship between husband and wife that is marriage."[66]

Reagan saw marriage as just that: a loving, lifelong relationship between a husband and a wife. For Reagan, that was marriage. Take careful note of his formulation: a loving, lifelong relationship between husband and wife *is* marriage. This, too, was one of those time-tested values—a value that conservatives needed to help conserve for the best of the culture and the country.

To modern eyes and ears, these Reagan statements might (and should) prompt thoughts about current efforts by liberals/progressives to redefine marriage by allowing for same-sex marriage. For the record, Ronald Reagan certainly never addressed the issue of "gay marriage," which was unthinkable in his time, though he did remark (disapprovingly) on homosexuality.[67] Any politician advocating such a thing in Reagan's time—whether a Democrat or Republican, a conservative or liberal or progressive or wild-eyed radical—would have been hauled off to a lunatic asylum as a public menace. Nonetheless, as these statements and further ones below illustrate, Reagan unwaveringly believed in and defended the traditional, time-tested, ancient, biblical, biological, natural understanding of family: a married man and a woman and their children.[68]

As to a religious understanding, Reagan in a November 1986 proclamation for National Family Week referred to the family as "with us from the dawn of human history" and pondered "what each of us can do as a father, daughter, mother, son, or grandparent—as a member of a family—to strengthen this divine institution."[69] This *divine institution*, in Reagan's mind, included a child that had both a dad and a mom. Taking this to an even higher level, Reagan looked to "that one holy family," Jesus, Mary, and Joseph, evoking the image of "the calm of one still night long ago and of a family—father, mother, and newborn child."[70] This literal divine institution, in Reagan's mind, included a child that had both a dad and a mom.

Reagan warned of "those forces that would weaken or destroy" the family. He pointed not only to "totalitarian [communist] societies" that "see in the family a natural enemy" but also to domestic forces in America that "erode the stability of the family and, particularly, the marital commitment."[71] He alerted Americans to beware of a government whose intervention undercut the family and marriage. Government, insisted Reagan, should first and foremost do no harm. This was so crucial to Reagan that he enunciated the warning in a formal executive order (September 1987) titled "The Family."[72]

Reagan cautioned against not only government action that would hurt the family—which, again, he defined as mother, father, and children—but also "cultural and legal forces undermining the well-being of families." He noted that in recent decades, "a host of new pressures" had placed "fresh strains" on the family. "Even though the family has proven to be the most durable of all institutions," said Reagan, "its vitality is not guaranteed under all conditions." Reagan issued that particular warning in his final proclamation for National Family Week, November 1988, where he again affirmed the hand of God in designing the family: "The family, the birth- and dwelling-place of natural and self-sacrificing love, is the first of all social contracts. Rooted in the designs of the Creator and reinforced through the wise devices of the law, the family is the sum of a nation's heritage and the heart of a nation's strength. It is, moreover, the original mirror of mankind's hope for a world founded on bonds of tradition and affection."[73]

The law, according to Reagan, should reinforce the Creator's design for the family. The traditional family is the original mirror of mankind's hope.

Again, same-sex marriage was not an issue in Ronald Reagan's time, but, given these sentiments, it is very difficult to imagine Reagan today suddenly contradicting himself and favoring a redefinition of marriage that rejected the traditional, natural, and Judeo-Christian model of one man and one woman that he so steadfastly championed throughout his presidency. For Reagan to embrace such a redefinition would be to repudiate everything he stood for.

A conservative conserves institutions like marriage and the family; a progressive changes them.

A father and mother, of course, physically unite in the creation, bearing, and rearing of children. Marriage has a unitive function and procreative function. Men and women who come together in marriage should be open to the potential creation of children. Reagan saw this, too, as divinely determined. The children that come from the male-female marriage union are "gifts from God," said Reagan, "made in God's image and likeness." Such was precisely "what America's parents through the centuries have known their youngsters to be." He said that parents should give their children not only "hope and opportunity for the future," but also "a realization of their God-given individual worth and dignity, the liberty that is their due as Americans and human beings, and the reverence, thanks, and obedience we owe the Almighty for making us His children."[74]

Also given their due in this equation were the American Founding Fathers. Reagan recognized the Founders for having recognized the role of the Almighty in bestowing the right to life. He said that the Founders' promise that "all men are created equal, that they are endowed by their Creator with certain unalienable Rights, that among these are Life, Liberty and the pursuit of Happiness," is a promise to parents, to families, to communities, and to the country—but most of all to the "children entrusted to us." America has a duty to its children to cherish and protect them and to respect their "innate dignity" and rights.[75]

At the same time, Reagan wasn't naïve to the struggles of children and families, having endured such trials himself, particularly a father who was often unemployed, was never (not once) able to buy the family a home, and had an alcohol problem—even as that father was a caring man. Reagan acknowledged that not all children are blessed with loving, affirming, and understanding parents: "Many youngsters suffer the effects of permissiveness, lack of guidance, drug and alcohol abuse, and absence of religious faith," said Reagan. "Fortunately, remedies for these ills do exist, and families and concerned citizens are doing all they can to guarantee a future of promise and fulfillment for their own children and for all our kids."[76]

It is worth pausing to note that Reagan did not utter these things simply as smart presidential politics—a way to curry favor with evangelicals, with the Moral Majority. To the contrary, Reagan said these things because he was a conservative, and conservatives should (if they are indeed conservatives) believe these things. In fact, Reagan had openly professed his faith in families long before he arrived in the Oval Office, and his lengthiest such orations were often shared with fellow conservatives.

"Families must continue to be the foundation of our nation," Reagan told CPAC in February 1977, four years prior to his presidency. "Families—not government programs—are the best way to make sure our children are properly nurtured, our elderly are cared for, our cultural and spiritual heritages are perpetuated, our laws are observed and our values are preserved." That being the case, government should most of all not damage families: "Thus it is imperative that our government's programs, actions, officials and social welfare institutions never be allowed to jeopardize the family. We fear the government may be powerful enough to destroy our families; we know that it is not powerful enough to replace them."[77]

Reagan also insisted that the Republican Party, the vehicle that he chose to drive conservatism to the White House, "must be committed to working always in the interest of the American family."[78]

Once thus in the White House, via his Republican Party nomination, Reagan continued to pitch the importance of the family. He did so to his fellow conservatives and to the nation generally. As to the former, he told CPAC in 1981, "Because ours is a consistent philosophy of government, we can be very clear: We do not have a social agenda, a separate economic agenda, and a separate foreign agenda. We have one agenda." That agenda included this bold statement: "Just as surely as we seek to put our financial house in order and rebuild our nation's defenses, so too we seek to protect the unborn, to end the manipulation of schoolchildren by utopian planners, and permit the acknowledgement of a Supreme Being in our classrooms just as we allow such acknowledgements in other public institutions."[79]

This was a common, core message from Reagan to conservatives about their shared philosophy. At CPAC in 1987, he made a similar statement:

> Modern conservatism is an active, not a reactive philosophy. It's not just in opposition to those vices that debase character and community, but affirms values that are at the heart of civilization. We favor protecting and strengthening the family, an institution that was taken for granted during the decades of liberal domination of American government. The family, as became clear in the not-too-distant past, is taken for granted at our peril. Victimized most were the least fortunate among us [the unborn], those who sorely needed the strength and protection of the family.[80]

Reagan said that the "real friends of the conservative movement" are those who not only support but also "aggressively" vote for "sound values" and "family values."[81]

But Reagan did not merely preach to the conservative choir. He took this homily to the nation. As quoted earlier, Reagan, as president, issued numerous statements and proclamations on the family, on parents, on children, on educators of children, and on a myriad of related issues. He wanted to speak to the wider American family, far beyond conservative brothers and sisters. Reagan even commissioned a special working group, ordered through Attorney General Ed Meese, who was acting chair of the White House Domestic Policy Council, to study how government could be more supportive (and less detrimental) to families. The report, presented by senior adviser Gary Bauer in December 1986, was titled *The Family: Preserving America's Future.* Above all, it affirmed Reagan's long-held principle that government at any level (federal, state, or local) should "first of all, do no harm." The report insisted that "government cannot abolish the family." Doing so would undermine "the social foundation of the state itself."

Among the hot-button family-related issues he tackled head-on, Reagan did not shy from discussing the taboo subject of sex. The 1980s was in the full throes of the sexual revolution. Reagan unhesitatingly staked some unwaveringly conservative claims. According to Reagan, both parents and educators alike should teach children not to engage in premarital sex. They should teach children to "place sexuality in the context of marriage, fidelity, commitment, and maturity." Reagan made this particular statement, incidentally, during a presidential proclamation declaring AIDS Awareness and Prevention Month.[82] He did not shirk from telling parents to teach chastity.[83] The family was a place of moral instruction: "The family is our school of conscience."[84]

If the family is not a place to nourish the conscience, then what is?

Finally, since moral instruction was a "primary responsibility" of parents,[85] according to Reagan, this also meant that American children should not be morally misguided by their public school system, especially one that indoctrinated children according to a certain political agenda, one that denied God and denied school prayer—as it also denied chastity. Families were the bedrock of America's religious and moral foundation. They had a role "in maintaining the spiritual strength of religious commitment among our people."[86]

In all, these vital social issues comprised a cohesive—and family-focused—conservative agenda. As a conservative, Reagan did not neglect these often controversial and politically explosive topics. Conservatism was an ideology for life, and thus it could not and cannot ignore such topics, even when politically sticky. And the family is the home and beating heart of conservatism.

It is difficult to overstate the profound importance of the family—mother, father, children—to Ronald Reagan's understanding of America and of conservatism.

Sanctity and Dignity of Human Life

As we saw in some of these comments, Reagan did not neglect the unborn child among those he included in the human family.[87]

At the heart of the relationship between family and faith and freedom is the human person. The human person has God and has freedom, and by definition exists; the person comes into existence through the union of a woman and a man—preferably, a mother and a father. A person cannot become a person, of course, if life is denied. Moreover, without a right to life, there can be no individual freedom or other rights. The right to life is the first and most fundamental of all human freedoms, without which other human freedoms literally cannot exist.

"My administration is dedicated to the preservation of America as a free land," said President Reagan in 1983. "And there is no cause more important for preserving that freedom than affirming the transcendent right to life of all human beings, the right without which no other rights have any meaning."[88]

For Reagan, that right to life began in the womb. It began at conception. As president, Reagan supported a Human Life

Amendment to the U.S. Constitution, which would have inserted into the Constitution these words: "The paramount right to life is vested in each human being from the moment of fertilization without regard to age, health or condition of dependency." He favored providing every human being—at all stages of development—protection as "persons" with the "right to life" under the Fourteenth Amendment.[89]

Reagan's respect for human life arguably began way back in the 1920s when the young man was a lifeguard for seven summers at the Rock River in Dixon, Illinois. He patrolled the murky, swift currents from ages fifteen through twenty-two. There, in that capacity, Ronald Reagan saved the lives of seventy-seven people. "One of the proudest statistics of my life is seventy-seven," he said many decades later.[90]

Generally, these experiences taught Reagan quite a bit about life. His later good friend Bill Clark, a kindred spirit in the pro-life cause, maintained that the lifeguarding instilled in the young man a basic respect for the sanctity and dignity of human life, which later manifested itself not only in President Reagan's opposition to abortion but also in his abhorrence of the prospect of nuclear war and empathy for the suffering citizens behind the Iron Curtain.[91]

Reagan's concern for life was also an outgrowth of his faith. The right to life was an issue he found inseparable from the life of Christ. In a January 1984 speech to religious broadcasters, he said, "God's most blessed gift to his family is the gift of life. He sent us the Prince of Peace as a babe in the manger."[92] Like nineteenth-century clergy who led the movement to abolish slavery, Reagan as a Christian saw himself as duty-bound to fight abortion, which he equated with slavery in terms of moral outrage and deprivation of human dignity. He made that analogy to the National Religious Broadcasters, quoting Jesus Christ in the process:

> This nation fought a terrible war so that black Americans
> would be guaranteed their God-given rights. Abraham
> Lincoln recognized that we could not survive as a free land

when some could decide whether others should be free or slaves. Well, today another question begs to be asked: How can we survive as a free nation when some decide that others are not fit to live and should be done away with? I believe no challenge is more important to the character of America than restoring the right to life to all human beings. Without that right, no other rights have meaning. "Suffer the little children to come unto me, and forbid them not, for such is the kingdom of God."[93]

Together, Reagan assured the religious broadcasters, he and they must convince their fellow countrymen that America "should, can, and will preserve God's greatest gift": the right to life. This was an evocative statement that did not escape criticism by pro-choice liberals in the media. In an editorial, the *New York Times* blasted Reagan for this analogy, insisting that the real modern "bondage" was "the law's refusal to let women decide whether or not to bear a child—until the Supreme Court read this basic liberty into the Constitution."[94]

Reagan did not care what the *New York Times* thought, especially given the gravity of the crime at hand. He was undeterred, raising the rhetoric higher still. In an especially high-profile occasion— his 1986 State of the Union address—Reagan lamented, "Today there is a wound in our national conscience. America will never be whole as long as the right to life granted by our Creator is denied to the unborn."[95]

Many such manifestations of Reagan's pro-life convictions could be cited here.[96] Yet, one particularly eloquent example has been missed in most biographical treatments:

In a July 1987 speech to a small group of pro-life leaders gathered at the White House, Reagan began: "[M]any of you, perhaps most, never dreamed of getting involved in politics. What brought you into politics was a matter of conscience, a matter of fundamental conviction ... Many of you have been attacked for being single-issue activists or single-issue voters. But I ask: What single issue could be of greater significance?" Reagan said that if one is unsure precisely when life begins, one should err in a way that protects rather than robs life: "If there's even a question about when human life begins, isn't it our duty to err on the side of life?"[97] And Reagan finished with this:

> I'd like to leave you with a quotation that means a great deal to me. These are the words of my friend, the late Terence Cardinal Cooke, of New York. "The gift of life, God's special gift, is no less beautiful when it is accompanied by illness or weakness, hunger or poverty, mental or physical handicaps, loneliness or old age. Indeed, at these times, human life gains extra splendor as it requires our special care, concern, and reverence. It is in and through the weakest of human vessels that the Lord continues to reveal the power of His love."[98]

Here was a warning against the pallbearers of the progressive death march, from Planned Parenthood founder and progressive/liberal icon Margaret Sanger—who hoped to expunge the gene pool of what she termed "human weeds" and "human waste" and "morons" and "idiots" and "imbeciles"[99]—to the euthanasia precipice to which America lurches. It starts with the weakest of vessels: the infant in its mother's womb. The dignity of that infant was, in Reagan's view, a reflection of the dignity God lent to man. It was vital that the unborn child be protected. Conservatives should never neglect these most vulnerable human vessels that need their help for life.

American Exceptionalism

Ronald Reagan also personified American exceptionalism. He was the preeminent spokesman for an exceptional America.[100]

Reagan glowingly described America as a "beacon" to all of humanity, as "the last best hope," a "Shining City upon a Hill." That nation would shine its light unto men, perched atop a mountain for the world to admire, a model for other nations to emulate. It signaled hope to those "captive peoples" behind the Iron Curtain.

Reagan was saying these things publicly three decades before he was elected president. Consider an instructive June 1952 commencement address he gave to tiny William Woods College (an all-women's college) in Fulton, Missouri, which he titled "America, the Beautiful." There, the forty-one-year-old Hollywood actor affirmed that America is "less of a place than an idea," a place that resided deep in the souls of men "ever since man started his long trail from the swamps." Stated Reagan,

> [The idea of America] is nothing but the inherent love of freedom in each one of us, and the great ideological struggle that we find ourselves engaged in today is not a new struggle. It's the same old battle. We met it under the name of Hitlerism; we met it under the name of Kaiserism; and we have met it back through the ages in the name of every conqueror that has ever set upon a course of establishing his rule over mankind. It is simply the idea, the basis of this country and of our religion, the idea of the dignity of man, the idea that deep within the heart of each one of us is something so God-like and precious that no individual or group has a right to impose his or its will upon the people so well as they can decide for themselves.

This was stirring enough, but then Reagan went further, telling the young women assembled that day, "I, in my own mind, have thought of America as a place in the divine scheme of things that was set aside as a promised land ... I believe that God in shedding his grace on this country has always in this divine scheme of things kept an eye on our land and guided it as a promised land."[101]

This, of course, is a picture of an exceptional America. Reagan summoned the image again and again until his final days, making no apologies for his passionate love of America.[102] Quite the contrary, he unabashedly retained the role of unflagging, flag-waving spokesman.

Importantly, Reagan's detractors often did not realize, or simply refused to concede, that Reagan was not arguing that America was without fault. His patriotism was not a jingoism or crude ultranationalism. Consider that in his most strident attack on the Soviet Union—his March 1983 "Evil Empire" speech—he first paused to point the finger inward at America for her past sins, especially slavery, racism, anti-Semitism, and "other forms of ethnic and racial hatred." "Our nation, too, has a legacy of evil with which it must deal," Reagan lamented. America was not perfect. Nonetheless, in Reagan's estimation America was, overall, in general, good, special, unique—yes, exceptional.

Alas, Reagan expressed this eloquently in his Farewell Address given from the Oval Office, where he explained what he meant all those years with his many reminisces of a "Shining City":

> The phrase comes from John Winthrop, who wrote it to describe the America he imagined. What he imagined was important because he was an early Pilgrim, an early freedom man. He journeyed here on what today we'd call a little wooden boat; and like the other Pilgrims, he was looking for a home that would be free. I've spoken of the Shining City all my political life, but I don't know if I ever quite communicated what I saw when I said it. But in my mind it was a tall, proud city built on rocks stronger than oceans, wind-swept, God-blessed, and teeming with people of all kinds living in harmony and peace; a city with free ports that hummed with commerce and creativity. And if there had to be city walls, the walls had doors and the doors were open to anyone with the will and the heart to get here. That's how I saw it, and see it still.

As later noted by Dr. Bill Bennett, Reagan's secretary of education, this Reagan statement was not only a parting presidential message but a history lesson, a chance to *educate* Americans about America rather than merely wave goodbye to Americans. It was a teachable moment in American exceptionalism.[103]

For that matter, Ronald Reagan also believed in the exceptionalism of the American people. He had an uncommon faith in common Americans. He had an unshakable optimism in their inherent goodness, wisdom, work ethic, and common sense. They could do anything; they could achieve anything. He was convinced of American ability and ingenuity.

Reagan had witnessed this in his own life, with his own achievements, evidenced by his plainly remarkable ability to succeed. Right out of college, his career quickly took off, a steady upward trajectory first into radio and then to Hollywood, thriving in both mediums at the height of their dominance. As to Hollywood, a critical period in Reagan's political formulation and in formulating his views on the exceptionalism of Americans was his work for *GE Theater* and its corporate sponsor, General Electric. In 1954, Reagan became host of *GE Theater*, a highly coveted job, where he would remain through 1962. It became one of the top shows on television, drawing the very best Hollywood talent.[104] But equally impressive was its impact on Reagan away from the camera. To promote the show, General Electric asked its popular host to travel the country to visit various facilities. Reagan happily toured GE plants, meeting with executives and employees and giving lunchtime and dinner speeches. He mingled with management and assembly workers alike, with white collars and blue collars. This interaction had a far-reaching effect on Reagan's political development and respect for the common man. The GE experience was a workshop for Reagan, a tutorial to the common man, an extended apprenticeship in the American people's can-do competence. It never left him, affirming and amplifying his faith in everyday Americans.[105]

Reagan was certain: If Americans put their minds to it, they could do anything. He took that conviction with him to the governorship of California and all the way to the White House. In his first inaugural address, Reagan closed with a tear in his eye and lump in his throat when imploring his fellow Americans:

"Together with God's help we can and will resolve the problems which now confront us. And after all, why shouldn't we believe that? We are Americans."[106]

Yes. Why shouldn't they? *They were Americans.* To Reagan, that meant everything. It said it all.

Reagan was also convinced, and said repeatedly, that if given all the facts, all the information, unbiased and unfiltered by the liberal press, Americans would make the best choice every time.

Reagan was thus convinced that when he directly addressed the American people, particularly in nationally televised addresses, he could convince them of good ideas. The key, for Reagan, was to go around the biased filter of the national news media. The Great Communicator craved a medium of direct communication with everyday Americans. Reagan's many Oval Office addresses provided that platform.

In his Farewell Address, Reagan noted that during his presidency he had earned that nickname, "The Great Communicator." But, countered Reagan, he never thought it was his style or the words he used that mattered most, that made him a great communicator; rather, he claimed, it was the content. He said: "I wasn't a great communicator, but I communicated great things." Those things, averred Reagan—who, for the record, *was* a great communicator— sprung from the soil of America: "they didn't spring full bloom from my brow, they came from the heart of a great nation—from our experience, our wisdom, and our belief in the principles that have guided us for two centuries." He insisted, "They called it the Reagan revolution. Well, I'll accept that, but for me it always seemed more like the great rediscovery, a rediscovery of our values and our common sense."[107]

Really, Reagan was saying, he was simply communicating America, which is less a place than an idea.

This was a job, incidentally, that Reagan saw as a duty of families. In his parting words from the Oval Office, he said that he wanted "an informed patriotism," and asked, "Are we doing a good enough job teaching our children what America is and what she represents in the long history of the world? Those of us who are over 35 or so years of age grew up in a different America. We were taught, very directly, what it means to be an American."[108]

Reagan feared "an eradication of the American memory that could result, ultimately, in an erosion of the American spirit. Let's start with some basics: more attention to American history and a greater emphasis on civic ritual."[109]

He hoped that not only educators but also parents would not fail at this essential civic task, a task he saw as quintessentially American. With a smile for his national audience, Reagan gently asked children to hold their parents accountable, chiding, "And let me offer lesson number one about America: All great change in America begins at the dinner table. So, tomorrow night in the kitchen I hope the talking begins. And children, if your parents haven't been teaching you what it means to be an American, let 'em know and nail 'em on it. That would be a very American thing to do."[110]

A very American thing to do. For Reagan, it was as American as a Shining City built on rocks stronger than oceans, wind-swept, God-blessed. An exceptional America. That's how Ronald Reagan saw it.[111]

The Founders' Wisdom and Vision

Reagan placed great faith not only in America and Americans but especially in the American Founders. It was the Founders' wisdom and vision that plowed the ground, combed the soil, and paved the way to American exceptionalism.

Throughout American history our presidents have invoked our nation's Founding Fathers. This, of course, includes recent presidents, from John F. Kennedy to Barack Obama, though Obama has acknowledged the Founders far less often and decidedly differently than his predecessors—referring to them, for instance, as "men of property and wealth."[112] The words of our Founders frequently have been resurrected in the rhetoric of our presidents. No modern president, however, cited the Founders as frequently and thematically as did Ronald Reagan.

When Reagan reached for the Founders, Americans learned a great deal not only about 1776 but also about where Ronald Reagan, as the nation's fortieth president during the 1980s, planned to lead the nation two hundred years later. Among all modern presidents, Reagan plainly rediscovered the American Founders. He called upon the Founders in a powerfully, wholly unique but appropriate way, and far more than any modern president—by leaps and bounds.

In researching this in the official *Public Papers of the Presidents of the United States*,[113] I found that Presidents Kennedy, Richard Nixon, Lyndon Johnson, and Bill Clinton all commonly cited the Founders, specifically within a range of about 100–200 times, with LBJ the highest at roughly 240. (Kennedy was approximately 160 and Nixon and Clinton around 100.) Yet, they all finish a distant second to Reagan, who cited the Founders some 850 times.

Some further comparisons: President George H. W. Bush cited the Founders roughly sixty times, and no president cited them as infrequently as Jimmy Carter and Gerald Ford, with Carter in the range of thirty-some citations and Ford with merely a handful. The sparseness of the Carter and Ford citations is especially odd given that their times in office occurred around America's bicentennial.

Among our recent presidents, the most frequently quoted Founders were Jefferson, Lincoln, and Washington, in that order. Reagan was no exception, acknowledging Jefferson nearly three hundred times, Lincoln more than two hundred times, and Washington almost two hundred times.

When Reagan did not mention the Founders by name, he mentioned their purposes. Most interesting, Reagan's "Founders" went back not only to 1776 but also to 1620, to 1630, to the Pilgrims, to John Winthrop and the crew of the *Arabella*, to William Penn.

Reagan went to the Founders on behalf of emphasizing the importance of limited government, the significance of faith to America and its people, and the inherited exceptionalism of America—as a "Shining City" with a special destiny for all mankind. In his own time, he portrayed a nation with a people facing another historic challenge two centuries beyond the American Revolution: a Cold War challenge. He borrowed the ideas and principles of the Founders in coloring a portrait of the American nation and system in this new challenging period. He contrasted that nation and its system with the totalitarian system of the USSR. And the America he portrayed to its people and the wider world in the 1980s was still the Founders' America. He evinced an abiding, ongoing patriotic and intellectual loyalty to their thoughts and vision. Their vision would sustain us still, in yet another challenge.

In short, Reagan connected his vision of government with that of the Founders. He concluded that at the axis of this unique place forged by those unique Founders was a basic understanding that the proper, fundamental function of government was to protect life, liberty, property, and the *pursuit* of happiness. Reagan's Founders were the authors and signers of a Constitution and Declaration that affirmed these basic principles of humanity—the First Amendment freedoms, the basic civil liberties, the nation's first principles.

As noted, Reagan's first nationally prominent speech was his October 27, 1964, "Time for Choosing" speech. It was given on behalf of Barry Goldwater's presidential candidacy and was nationally televised. While conservatives recognize the speech for launching Reagan as a viable political figure, and for his heralding a "rendezvous with destiny," often neglected is how Reagan, in that address, harkened back to the spirit of 1776—long before he sought the Republican presidential bid in 1976.

Reagan immediately followed up the speech by laying out that same sense of destiny in a 1965 memoir intended to more fully introduce him and his political thinking to the voting public. Titled *Where's the Rest of Me?*, the book finished with a revealing rhetorical flourish. In its final paragraphs—which borrowed from his 1960s speeches, including a heavy excerpt from the "Time for Choosing" address—lay the logic that would also compel Reagan to forcefully reject the coming policy of détente with the Soviet Union in the 1970s:

> We are told that the problem is too complex for a simple answer. They are wrong. There is no easy answer, but there is a simple answer. We must have the courage to do what we know is morally right, and this policy of accommodation asks us to accept the greatest possible immorality. We are being asked to buy our safety from the threat of the [atomic] bomb by selling into permanent slavery our fellow human beings enslaved behind the Iron Curtain. To tell them to give up their hope of freedom because we are ready to make a deal with their slave masters.[114]

Reagan was referring to freedom at home and abroad. On the latter, he rejected any détente-based "deal" whereby the United States accommodated the USSR and sold into "permanent slavery" those Eastern European captives behind the Iron Curtain. Such deals were not simply wrong and immoral but were also the "greatest possible immorality." Insisting that a nation that chose such a course was opting for "disgrace," the future president issued a dire statement that (as usual) included moving images from the Founders:

> Alexander Hamilton warned us that a nation which can prefer disgrace to danger is prepared for a master and deserves one. Admittedly, there is a risk in any course we follow. Choosing the high road cannot eliminate that risk … Should Moses have told the children of Israel to live in slavery rather than dare the wilderness? Should Christ have refused the Cross? Should the patriots at Concord Bridge have refused to fire the shot heard round the world? Are we to believe that all the martyrs of history died in vain?

Reagan concluded that Americans must choose "courage" over accommodation. He told his compatriots that he and they had a rendezvous with destiny. Together they could preserve for their children "this, the last best hope of man on earth," or they could "sentence them to take the first step into a thousand years of darkness." If they tried but failed, said Reagan dramatically, at least their children and children's children could "say of us that we justified our brief moment here. We did all that could be done." At the very least, this meant summoning the moral courage to reject accommodation with slave masters if and when such deals reared their cowardly heads.

For America, and for Reagan, the first such case and test of moral courage began in 1776, and the Founders accepted and passed that test, and then changed the world. It was a lingering lesson for Americans for all time, not just a history lesson about their past but also about their future. It was a lesson for Reagan.

To that end, throughout his career, Reagan would find special inspiration in these words of Founder Thomas Paine: "We have it in our power to begin the world all over again."[115] Reagan called upon those words of Paine over and over again.

To Reagan, the American founding was not just about a group of people, a group of men. The American founding was about the establishment and institutionalization of *ideas*: a vision and understanding of America and the very essence of constitutional government, a representative republic, and the powerful concept of being endowed by our Creator with certain unalienable rights.

Sadly, that noble ideal, that truly commendable vision and wisdom, has not been a dominant element of the ideals, vision, wisdom, and rhetoric of all of our modern presidents, or of recent presidential candidates. Issues are important, yes, but issues come and go. America as an idea is timeless. If America's presidents, or potential presidents, do not know this or do not articulate it, then they have blown a golden opportunity, a golden patrimony. The president can teach as well as lead. The president's rhetoric is the wellspring of his bully pulpit. What kind of rhetoric will the president use?

For Ronald Reagan, it was frequently the Founders' rhetoric. By consistently and unashamedly articulating the founding and its first principles, Ronald Reagan was, in effect, behaving like a teacher as well as a leader. His presidency offered, in many ways, an enduring civics lesson. The Great Communicator communicated the founding. What he said is worth remembering and worth teaching all over again.

Lower Taxes

From a richer philosophical perspective, Reagan conservatism is about the Founders' wisdom and vision. From a modern policy perspective, Reagan conservatism is first and foremost about reducing the size of government and, especially, the mother's milk that sustains government: federal taxes. Ronald Reagan wanted to reduce the level of taxation, and most notably federal income tax rates.[116]

Speaking of which, in 1913, progressives struck gold. That year, they achieved a stunning victory, permanently establishing a federal income tax. This huge change was made possible by a historic amendment to the Constitution (the Sixteenth Amendment), ratified February 3, 1913, and by the pen of the progressive's progressive, President Woodrow Wilson, who signed the tax into law on October 3, 1913. It was a major political victory for Wilson and fellow progressives then and still today.

The notion of taxing income in America was not completely new. Such taxes existed before, albeit temporarily, at very small levels, and for national emergencies like war. The idea of a permanent tax for permanent income redistribution broke new ground in America. The only debate was the exact percentage of the tax. In no time, progressives learned they could never get enough.

In 1913, when the progressive income tax began, the top rate was a mere 7 percent, applied only to the fabulously wealthy (incomes above $500,000). By the time Woodrow Wilson left office in 1921, the progressive icon had hiked the upper rate to 73 percent. World War I (which, for America, went from 1917 to 1918) had given Wilson a short-term justification, but so did Wilson's passion for a robust "administrative state."

Rivaling Wilson in his appetite for government was another progressive champion, President Franklin Delano Roosevelt, who exploded the upper-income rate to a staggering 94 percent. Incredibly, FDR once considered a top rate of 99.5 percent on income above $100,000.[117]

One person who was fed up with these confiscatory rates was an actor in Hollywood who called himself a progressive FDR Democrat: Ronald Reagan. Reagan came to see the counterproductive nature of these excessive taxes. He thought the top rates so punitive that they discouraged work, including his own. The so-called B movie actor was one of the top box-office draws at Warner Brothers. Reagan saw no incentive in continuing to work—that is, make more movies—once his income hit the top rate. He realized who suffered from that choice. It wasn't Reagan; he was wealthy. It was the custodians, cafeteria ladies, camera crew, and working folks on the studio lot. They lost work. They lost money.

Reagan was appalled. In speeches in the 1950s and 1960s, he blasted the progressive income tax as "right out of" Karl Marx's *Communist Manifesto*. Indeed, the *Manifesto* calls for "a heavy progressive or graduated income tax." It is point two in Marx's ten-point program, second only to his call for "abolition of property."[118]

Reagan viewed such rates—and the government beast that they fed—as symptomatic of what he called "creeping socialism." He decried what he perceived as the growing permanency of the welfare state. He came to believe that many of the relief programs that FDR instituted during the Great Depression were "necessary measures during an emergency" but, unfortunately, had instead "trapped families forever on a treadmill of dependency."[119] Those programs became permanent and held recipients down rather than helping them up. The once-proud FDR Democrat became increasingly exasperated with the Democratic Party's warm embrace and hearty expansion of those programs. With LBJ's Great Society ratcheting up the "nanny state" further still, Reagan forever parted ways with the Democratic Party.

To Reagan, the Democratic Party had once been the party of the working man. Now it was becoming the party of the welfare man. He saw no light at the end of the Democratic tunnel.

"I didn't leave the Democratic Party," Reagan would famously assert. "The Democratic Party left me."

The Great Society vigorously continued the seemingly unstoppable growth of government bureaucracy. The administrative state that had taken flight with Woodrow Wilson and the progressives took a giant leap forward under FDR, a further extension still under LBJ, and continued to grow under Presidents Richard Nixon (a Republican) and Jimmy Carter (a Democrat). As to Nixon and Carter, entirely new areas fell under federal control, as energy, the environment, and education came within the greedy grip of federal planners—all were centralized under new agencies and departments. Practically every new presidential administration brought more administrative agencies—more bureaucracies. It seemed like the only certainty was government growth. Reagan quipped that the only guarantee of eternal life in this world is a government bureaucracy.

By the 1970s, when he was a presidential candidate, Ronald Reagan believed that out-of-control government growth, spending, regulation, and taxes had sapped the American economy of its vitality, and particularly its ability to bounce back after a recession. The economy needed to be freed in order to perform. "As government expands," observed Reagan, "liberty contracts."[120]

The prescription that Reagan recommended rested on four pillars: tax cuts, deregulation, reductions in the rate of growth of government spending, and a stable, carefully managed growth of the money supply.[121] He wanted to stimulate economic growth via tax cuts, allowing the American people to keep their money and spend and invest it more wisely and efficiently than government could; this was, in effect, private-sector stimulus—a stark contrast from President Obama's massive $800 billion public-sector "stimulus" in 2009. Among Reagan's various tax cuts, the federal income tax reduction was the centerpiece. Reagan secured a 25 percent across-the-board reduction in tax rates over a three-year period (5 percent, 10 percent, 10 percent), beginning in October 1981. Eventually, through these and later cuts, the upper-income marginal tax rate was dropped from 70 percent to 28 percent.

In the process, Reagan also dramatically simplified the tax code. When he was inaugurated, there were sixteen separate tax brackets, each applied to varying levels of income. When Reagan was finished, there were only two brackets.[122] Not only did this simplification eliminate complexity, but it also eliminated loopholes and removed some four million working poor from the tax rolls; they no longer paid any federal income tax.[123]

Liberals in the Obama era have persistently argued that Reagan (like Obama) "increased taxes." They are either ignorant of the facts or deliberately obfuscating the issue. Reagan indeed occasionally compromised with Democrats (who controlled Congress) on tax increases in order to pass a budget. For instance, Reagan agreed to increase excise taxes (on gasoline) in 1982, the Social Security payroll tax in 1983, and smaller tax rises in 1984 and 1987. His willingness to compromise came in exchange for promised spending cuts, which Reagan hoped would thereby reduce the deficit. In 1982, Congressional Democrats promised Reagan spending cuts in exchange for a tax increase by a ratio of three to one. It seemed like a superb deal, but the promised cuts never came.[124]

Significantly, however, these tax increases did not involve *income* taxes. As Reagan biographer Steve Hayward notes, Reagan "never budged an inch on marginal income tax rates."[125] Reagan understood that not all taxes, or tax increases, are equal.

Ultimately, Reagan presided over the largest tax cut in American history, and accomplished it working in tandem with (rather than against) a huge Democratic Party majority in the House. It was a bipartisan triumph. The *Washington Post* called Reagan's accomplishment "one of the most remarkable demonstrations of presidential leadership in modern history."

After a slow start through 1982–1983, the stimulus effect of the Reagan tax cuts was extraordinary, sparking the longest peacetime expansion/recovery in the nation's history: ninety-two consecutive months, far surpassing the previous record of fifty-eight months. The bogeymen of the 1970s—chronic unemployment and the deadly combination of double-digit inflation and interest rates— were vanquished. The poverty rate dropped. Incomes (median earnings) and standard of living jumped up. The Dow Jones Industrial Average, which, in real terms, had declined by 70 percent from 1967 through 1982, nearly tripled from 1983 through 1989. The telecom and computer industries began their eventual explosion in the 1990s.[126]

Contrary to liberal demonology, women and blacks and other minorities did extremely well during the Reagan years. Real income for a median black family had dropped 11 percent from 1977 through 1982; from 1982 through 1989, coming out of the recession, it rose by 17 percent. In the 1980s, there was a 40 percent jump in the number of black households earning $50,000 or more. Black unemployment (which has increased significantly under President Barack Obama) actually fell faster than white unemployment in the 1980s. The number of black-owned businesses increased by almost 40 percent, while the number of blacks who enrolled in college increased by almost 30 percent (white college enrollment increased by only 6 percent).[127]

There were likewise impressive numbers for Hispanics, who saw similar (if not higher) increases in family income, employment, and college enrollment. Among these, the number of Hispanic-owned businesses in the 1980s grew by an astounding 81 percent, and the number of Hispanics enrolled in college jumped 45 percent.[128]

Liberals love to emphasize the income gap between men and women. Well, under Reagan, women went from earning 60 cents for every dollar a man earned to 71 cents, and their employment and median earnings both outpaced their male counterparts'. Women enrolled in college in record numbers.[129]

Liberals tried to blame Reagan (and still do) for the homeless in the 1980s. They did so with hysteria and a viciousness and recklessness. With the help of their media, their castigations had notable success, mainly because the matter of trying to quantify the total number of homeless (and the reasons for their plight) is extremely complicated.[130] For one, the homeless do not register like the unemployed do, or like those filing for welfare benefits. Calculating the homeless requires careful study. In the 1980s, the Department of Housing and Urban Development (HUD) attempted to do just that. Homeless advocates like the late Mitch Snyder spoke of millions upon millions of homeless (three million, claimed Snyder) stacked like cordwood and wasting away on the streets. One account ridiculously claimed 250,000 homeless in Chicago alone, which the press dutifully reported. In 1984, HUD released its report, estimating 250,000–350,000 homeless. That was the data going into Reagan's fourth year, as the Reagan expansion was mushrooming. Even by the late 1980s, most studies placed the homeless around 300,000.[131]

(By comparison, the number of homeless under Barack Obama by his fourth year was double the number under Reagan. At the time of my writing, the most recent study is a report by the National Alliance to End Homelessness, titled *State of Homelessness in America 2012*.[132] That report listed 636,017 homeless. Unlike Reagan's reelection, the press was completely silent on the homeless under Obama. It was a complete nonissue. Of related interest, the number of Americans on food stamps under Reagan was reduced to 18 million, compared to a record

48 million under Obama, a shocking 43% increase from his first year as president.[133])

Ronald Reagan did not create the homeless. In fact, it is difficult to know if the number of homeless even increased under Reagan. Nonetheless, as Professor Andrew Busch notes, "If the number of homeless actually did increase in the 1980s—and may well have—it was not because of cuts in federal housing programs." Busch notes that federal housing expenditures under Reagan actually increased sizably in the 1980s, by 58 percent, and the number of subsidized housing units rose by a huge amount: from 3.3 million to 4.3 million. And this was despite decreases in poverty rates and unemployment.[134]

Overall, the "Reagan boom" not only produced widespread prosperity but—along with the attendant Soviet collapse—helped generate budget surpluses in the 1990s. Carter-Ford-era terms like "malaise" and "misery index" vanished. Only during the Obama years, and specifically in 2011, has America reapproached similar misery-index levels, reaching a twenty-eight-year high.[135]

Finally, aside from the matter of the economic impact of the tax cuts, it is important to understand that tax cuts were the very essence of Reaganomics. Reagan conservatism, in the realm of economic policy, is first and foremost about tax cuts.

Limited Government

In reducing taxes, Ronald Reagan also wanted to reduce government to a more limited role. By 1981, Reagan concluded, government was involved in or doing far more than it should.

Reagan conservatism, and conservatism generally, is often misunderstood as antigovernment. It is not. Conservatives believe that government has a role in preserving freedom and order and providing certain services. Conservatives are willing to use government to promote the common good of the citizenry, and even (at times) to protect citizens from themselves. Thus, for instance, conservatives are against the legalization of certain societal vices, from prostitution to gambling to drugs, just to name a few.

Ronald Reagan, in line with traditional conservative thinking, was not antigovernment, but anti-*big* government. He was against unnecessary government, intrusive government, overly burdensome government, "nanny state" cradle-to-grave government, ever-expanding and encroaching government, unlimited government. Reagan favored limited government. As he said in his first inaugural address, "it's not my intention to do away with government."[136]

Admittedly, Reagan's push to downsize the federal government often got confused as plainly antigovernment—and Reagan himself helped foster that perception. An often-quoted Reagan quip was this line: "The nine most terrifying words in the English language are: 'I'm from the government and I'm here to help.'"

What Reagan was trying to humorously express, however, was his view that the federal government frequently worsens things where it shouldn't be involved in the first place. Reagan believed heartily that things better left to the private sector ought to be left to the private sector. In his "Time for Choosing" speech, he insisted that "outside of its legitimate functions, government does nothing as well or as economically as the private sector of the economy."

Reagan felt that by January 1981, when he was inaugurated, the federal government had subsumed far too many roles and duties that should have been left to the private sector or to local and state governments. As noted, he believed that FDR saw the New Deal as merely a "temporary measure" during a time of "national emergency." He speculated that FDR would not have advocated a permanent cradle-to-grave system that deterred so many Americans from financial independence and prosperity. Again, Reagan felt that this had only gotten worse—much worse—with LBJ's Great Society. All of these liberal "good intentions" had merely helped foster a "dependency class." And as government grew, so did tax rates to fuel the federal Leviathan. When Reagan invoked the mantra of "freedom," it was about freedom not only from Soviet/communist tyranny abroad, but also from out-of-control big government at home.

By 1981, in his self-written inaugural address, Reagan would state: "In this present crisis, government is not the solution to our problem; government *is* the problem."[137] (This is a far cry from Barack Obama's "only government" statement in February 2009, after his first inauguration. "The federal government is the only entity left with the resources to jolt our economy back into life," said Obama. "It is only government that can break the vicious cycle where lost jobs lead to people spending less money which leads to even more layoffs.") Note that Reagan did not say that government is *always* the problem but that, in the "present crisis," it was the problem. In Reagan's view, American government, by 1981, two hundred–plus years after the signing of the Declaration of Independence, had become too big; it had become the problem. Reagan wanted to return the nation to a more limited government that scaled back the welfare/entitlement state and returned to a better balance between federal and state government.

And so, to what degree did he succeed or fail in that endeavor?

On the plus side, the *Federal Register* was appreciably smaller after eight years of the Reagan presidency. The *Federal Register* is the official record/journal of the U.S. government's existing rules and regulations as well as proposed changes to rules and regulations. It is a compilation of all acts by the federal government, collected by the Office of the Federal Register. In short, the *Federal Register* is the preeminent record of federal regulations. The more rules and regulations, the larger and more intrusive the government.

In 1980, the year before Reagan entered the presidency, there were 87,012 pages in the Federal Register; by 1986, the Reagan administration had reduced the number to 47,418. The register included 21,092 pages of rules in 1980; by 1987, the Reagan administration reduced them to a low of 13,625. In 1980, there were 16,276 pages of proposed rules; by 1988, the number was 13,883.[138]

This scaling back of regulations was a definite Reagan success. What about federal spending in the 1980s? This is a more complicated question.

If looking at spending as a percentage of GDP, the Reagan numbers appear good. For instance, from 1980 to 1988 there was a consistent decline in discretionary domestic spending as a percentage of GDP. There was also a decline in programmatic mandatory spending (entitlement programs) as a percentage of GDP; specifically, programmatic mandatory spending was 10.4 percent of GDP in 1980 and 9.8 percent of GDP in 1989 (though it did increase in the mid-1980s). There was also a decline in discretionary nondefense spending as a percentage of GDP, which went from 5.2 percent of GDP in 1980 to 3.4 percent in 1989 (the final Reagan budget).[139]

Of course, GDP under Reagan increased significantly—which was a very healthy sign of economic prosperity. Yes, spending went down as a percentage of GDP, but spending in real dollars was a much bigger problem. For instance, entitlement spending decreased as a percentage of GDP, but it exploded in real dollars.[140]

Almost across the board, Reagan was unable to cut spending where he wanted. Unfortunately, this meant that Reagan was unable to cut the budget deficit, which was one of his greatest regrets.

Here, too, however, the issue is not as black and white as some would like.[141] For starters, President Reagan inherited chronic deficits. Since FDR, the budget had been balanced only a handful of times, mainly under President Eisenhower. From 1981 to 1989, the deficit under Reagan increased from $79 billion to $153 billion. In Reagan's defense, the deficit as a percentage of GDP barely moved; in fact, it was almost identical to when Reagan was elected: In 1980, the deficit was 2.7 percent of GDP; in 1989, it was 2.8 percent.[142] Again, however, that number is somewhat misleading because economic growth was so superb.

The worst years for the Reagan deficit were the mid-1980s.

The deficit peaked in the 1983–1986 period, hitting a high of $221 billion. Yet, as the economy continued to grow, the deficit declined, dropping sharply to $149 billion in 1987. The drop was aided by a revenue surge. From 1986 to 1987, revenue to the federal Treasury accelerated by a huge $85 billion, far outpacing spending, which increased only $14 billion.[143]

Liberal critics like to blame the Reagan tax cuts for an alleged lack of revenue that (in their view) contributed to the deficits. This is inaccurate. Reagan's tax cuts were not accompanied by a decline in revenue. Tax revenues under Reagan rose from $599 billion in 1981 to nearly $1 trillion in 1989. The problem was that outlays (i.e., government spending) all along outpaced revenues, soaring from $678 billion in 1981 to $1.143 trillion in 1989.

So, what was the culprit for the Reagan deficits?

The cause of the Reagan deficits was twofold: 1) the initial sharp drop in tax revenue due to the 1982–1983 recession and 2) excessive overall spending. And, yes, the perpetrator was not just social spending by Congressional Democrats but Reagan defense spending designed to take down the Soviet Union.[144] The defense spending, however, was a bargain of epic proportions. It helped kill a truly "Evil Empire" and win the Cold War, paving the way for Democrat President Bill Clinton and the Republican Congress in the 1990s to balance the budget with massive defense cuts (and a growing economy). Reagan biographer Lou Cannon has aptly called Reagan's deficits "war-time deficits."

As further indication of why liberals cannot blame Reagan's deficits on tax cuts, consider this: The peak period of Reagan's deficits was 1983–1986, when the upper income tax rate was still 50 percent, reduced to that level (from 70 percent) by Reagan's 1981 Economic Recovery Act. The rate was not reduced again until 1987, when it came down to 38.5 percent. The upper rate did not come down to 28 percent until 1988. And Reagan's deficits actually decreased in the 1987–1989 period, contrary to their increase in the 1983–1986 period.[145]

Think about the implications of this for current policy: The peak period of Reagan deficits occurred when the upper tax rate was 50 percent, far higher than the 39.6 percent rate that President Barack Obama and liberal Democrats demanded (for purposes of deficit reduction) in 2012–2013. If President Obama and fellow liberals believe the deficit will come down with a 39.6 percent rate, then why did it not go down with Reagan's 50 percent rate?

This gets back to the main reason for Reagan's deficits and for most deficits, whether a nation, a local government, a federal government, a home, a business, or whatever: excessive spending—that is, spending more money than you have. Any conservative should know that that's a recipe for imprudence and insolvency. A conservative favors limited government, which, by its very nature, must be a foe of deficits and debt.

Peace Through Strength

While Reagan wanted to cut government spending across the board, defense was a major exception. That thinking was a by-product of his times and his plans for America in the Cold War. To that end, another core element of Reagan conservatism was what he called "peace through strength."

Reagan long maintained that a buildup in U.S. military strength would decrease the likelihood of war and increase the likelihood of peace. It would also, he predicted, bring the Soviet Union to the negotiating table to reduce nuclear missile arsenals. America needed to build up its weaponry before both superpowers could build down. Thus, Reagan believed that heightened defense spending was worthwhile even if it heightened the overall budget deficit. The trade-off justified the cost.

"[W]hile we work for peace among men of good will," said Reagan in July 1968, then still a governor, "we must rebuild and maintain our strength; building peace will take time and strength is the currency which can buy that time."[146] In a June 1972 statement, he added, "National defense is not a threat to peace; it is the guarantee of peace with freedom."[147]

There are many such quotations from Reagan in this pre-presidential period, too numerous to list here.[148] One of the better testimonies was a May 1976 interview he did with *U.S. News & World Report*. Said Reagan,

> I think we have to make darn sure that we improve our military position to the point that we're not second best [to the Soviet Union], so that we can be truly dealing for peace through strength … If the U.S. would do this and the Soviets see this demonstration of will, they might say: "Oh, wait a minute. If we're going to keep up an arms race, this is going to go on forever and we can't catch them or match them." Then I think you could have legitimate reduction of arms. My belief is that the Soviet Union right now is surging ahead because it sees no intent on the part of our people to do this.[149]

Once sworn in as president, Reagan wasted no time translating this thinking into policy, and expressing it to the American people. "We will maintain sufficient strength to prevail if need be," he stated in his January 1981 inaugural, "knowing that if we do so we have the best chance of never having to use that strength."[150] Six months later, in a June press conference, he added, "I have to believe that our greatest goal must be peace, and I also happen to believe that that will come through our maintaining enough strength that we can keep the peace."[151] Similarly, in an October 19, 1981, speech at Yorktown, Reagan stated, "Military inferiority does not avoid a conflict, it only invites one and then ensures defeat … We're rebuilding our defenses so that our sons and daughters never need to be sent to war."[152] In a February 1983 speech in St. Louis, Reagan remarked, "There have been four wars in my lifetime. We didn't get in any of them because we were too strong."[153]

To achieve nuclear missile reductions with the Soviets, Reagan believed that peace through strength was a necessary prerequisite. He later stated, "[I]t was obvious that if we were ever going to get anywhere with the Russians in persuading them to reduce armaments, we had to bargain with them from *strength*, not weakness. If you were going to approach the Russians with a dove of peace in one hand, you had to have a sword in the other."[154]

Reagan hoped this would not merely bring the Soviets to the negotiating table but also challenge them to an arms race they could not afford—and would bankrupt themselves trying. Of course, many people believe that precisely that ultimately took place.

Importantly, this desire to bring the Soviets to the table for missile reductions reflects another core conviction of Ronald Reagan: He detested nuclear weapons. Contrary to the left's vile caricature of him as a trigger-happy nuclear warmonger, Reagan was horrified at the prospects of nuclear war. He so badly wanted to reduce the nuclear threat that he actually favored a total abolition of nuclear weapons, a position vigorously rejected not only by many of his advisers but also by many liberal Democrats who advocated a policy of mutual-assured destruction (MAD) that they believed lessened the risk of a nuclear exchange.

As scholars like Paul Lettow and Beth Fischer have detailed at length, Reagan was a "nuclear abolitionist."[155] What liberals did not understand—but should have, as Reagan made it abundantly clear in ubiquitous statements[156]—was that Reagan pursued a military buildup, including of certain nuclear weapons (such as the Pershing IIs / INFs), in order to prompt the Soviets to sign agreements that ultimately eliminated missiles on both sides. Again, that military strength could produce peace—in this case, it could produce a diminished threat of nuclear war.

But even apart from grand Cold War strategy, or wanting to reduce the nuclear threat, Reagan believed in military strength for its own sake, for keeping and advancing peace. This was a broader strength that went beyond the USSR and the Cold War to other enemies, whether in Europe or the Western Hemisphere or the Middle East. And in that sense, Reagan's "peace through strength" thinking has ongoing application still today, if not always.

Anti-communism

Peace through strength was needed to repel the communist threat, which was a threat at multiple levels. To Reagan, communism was the antithesis of freedom, faith, the family, the sanctity and dignity of human life, the Founders' vision and wisdom, lower taxes, and limited government. As Reagan put it, "Totalitarian communism is an absolute enemy of human freedom."[157]

Few things so typified Reagan quite like his stalwart anticommunism. It had long been part of his life; in fact, the bookends of Reagan's life were the rise of the Bolshevik Revolution and the fall of the Soviet Union (1917–1991). Communism was the ideology he confronted for a century. An extended line of quotations could here be marshaled to illustrate the point. A few are worth pondering:

In a May 1975 radio commentary, given between his years as governor and president, Reagan called communism a "disease." "Mankind has survived all manner of evil diseases and plagues," conceded Reagan, "but can it survive communism?" This disease had been "hanging on" for a half century or more. Reagan wanted Americans to know "just how vicious" communism "really is." For good measure, he added that "Communism is neither an economic or a political system—it is a form of insanity."[158]

To characterize communism as a disease might have struck some as hysterical commie bashing. Yet, in reality, it is hard to find many contagions that have silenced so many lives in such short time. In the twentieth century, probably the biggest killer among disease was the influenza epidemic of 1918–1919, which may have taken upwards of twenty-plus million worldwide, nowhere near the toll of the "disease" of communism, which took the lives of 100–140 million between 1917 and 1991.[159] The combined death tolls of World Wars I and II, the two deadliest wars in history, comprise only half the death toll committed by communism.

For Reagan, the rampant death alone was bad enough. Worse was the Soviet goal of expanding this deadly ideology worldwide. In 1975, he complained, "The Russians have told us over and over again their goal is to impose their incompetent and ridiculous system on the world." In July 1982, as president, he said that the USSR's "self-proclaimed goal is the domination of every nation on Earth." He reaffirmed these warnings in formal speeches, on the stump, in interviews—wherever he had the opportunity.[160]

Thus, Reagan sought to facilitate the end of what he termed an "Evil Empire," no less than "the focus of evil in the modern world." That desire, as he himself said, was motivated in part by his belief that as a Christian he was "enjoined by Scripture" to resist and attack evil wherever it lurked.[161] He saw his confrontation with communism as a spiritual one. He told a joint session of the Irish National Parliament on June 4, 1984, that the "struggle between freedom and totalitarianism today" was ultimately not a test of arms or missiles "but a test of faith and spirit." It was, he said, a "spiritual struggle."[162]

Reagan had his reasons, ranging from communism's vast casualties and expansionary ambitions to its intellectual bankruptcy and wholesale repression of basic civil liberties—religion, conscience, press, assembly, speech, travel, and emigration, just for starters. Communist governments erected cement walls and barbed wire to keep people from fleeing. Patrolling the walls and wire were their own soldiers, trained to shoot and kill any freedom-seekers desperately desiring a better life. Communist nations were maintained like prison cells.

Among the many forms of repression, Reagan was particularly aghast at communism's assault on religion. Soviet communists pursued what Mikhail Gorbachev later correctly called a "war on religion."[163] Marx himself had called religion the "opiate of the masses" and said that "communism begins where atheism begins."[164] The Bolsheviks' brutally atheistic godfather, Vladimir Lenin, declared that "there is nothing more abominable than religion," which he called "a necrophilia." Lenin analogized Christianity to venereal disease, and established formal government groups like the League of the Militant Godless. Speaking on behalf of the Bolshevik state, he declared in 1920, "We ... do not believe in God." Lenin later boasted that as a teenager, he had ripped the cross that hung from his neck and "tossed it into the rubbish bin."[165]

That was a metaphor for what Lenin's Bolshevik state did to religious believers for seventy years. They blew up churches— those they didn't transform into atheist museums or morph into some other twisted secular or state purpose. They imprisoned nuns in special sections of the gulag with prostitutes, deeming them "whores to Christ." They ridiculed priests and bishops in show trials, locked them up, drugged them, tormented and tortured them, and executed untold numbers, typically with bullets to the back of the head.

Worse still, the Soviets in turn forcibly exported this militant godlessness to all the communist satellites in their empire, brutalizing religious believers in historically devout nations around the world. Communism's endemic religious hatred went global. This armed assault on religious faith was aimed not just at Christians—Protestants, Catholics, Eastern Orthodox—but also against Jews, Muslims, Buddhists, and other faiths. For every persecuted Cardinal Wyszynski in Poland, Cardinal Mindszenty in Hungary, or Richard Wurmbrand in Romania, there was a Natan Sharansky or Walter Ciszek in Russia, a Severian Baranyk in the Ukraine, a Mojaddedi clan in Afghanistan, a Methodist missionary or follower of the Dalai Lama in China, a jailed nun in Cuba, or a Buddhist monk forced to renounce his vows in Cambodia. Whether the despot was Mao Tse-tung or Fidel Castro or Pol Pot or Joseph Stalin, the sentiment was the same: Religion was contemptible and must be destroyed. This was an unholy crusade for communists. They quibbled over the details of how to implement Marx's overall vision, but they were unanimous in one thing: Religion was the enemy.

As for Reagan, driven as he was by the "twin beacons" of faith and freedom, he was aghast at the communist war on religion. He saw himself as a voice for the voiceless in the communist world, those captive peoples languishing in the "heart of darkness." He unhesitatingly labeled the Soviet empire an "Evil Empire."

When Reagan did so, his courageous candor and expression of undeniable truth was met with revulsion. Liberals blasted his (alleged) saber rattling and bellicosity.[166] Nonetheless, Reagan held firm. In later defending himself for having dared to utter the truth about Soviet communism, he explained, "For too long our leaders were unable to describe the Soviet Union as it actually was ... I've always believed, however, that it's important to define differences."[167]

And what were those differences? Said Reagan, "The Soviet system over the years has purposely starved, murdered, and brutalized its own people. Millions were killed; it's all right there in the history books. It put other citizens it disagreed with into psychiatric hospitals, sometimes drugging them into oblivion. Is the system that allowed this not evil? Then why shouldn't we say so?"[168]

Reagan did say so. And he had said so from the beginning of his public life: There was no greater enemy to human freedom than communism.

Belief in the Individual

Lastly, at the hub of all these Reagan beliefs was his respect for the individual, whether the person suffering in the gulag, the person growing in the womb, the person paying taxes, the person caught on the treadmill of welfare-state dependency, the mom or dad or child who form the family, the farmer who produces food, the inventor who innovates, or the entrepreneur who starts a business and generates prosperity. Reagan was confident in the individual's ability to make a difference, to pick up himself or herself, to make and mirror America's exceptionalism, to change the world. He saw that power in his own life, his own family, his own career, his own ambition. The promise and freedom of individual action propelled America to dizzying achievements. He saw it. He knew it. He believed it.

For the record, this emphasis on the individual and individual action poses another marked contrast with the current president of the United States, Barack Obama, who speaks admiringly of what he calls "collective action," our "collective shoulder," and even "collective salvation," all fundamental to his belief in "redistributive change." The word *collective* appears frequently in President Obama's rhetoric, including in his memoirs, *Dreams from My Father*, where he pondered "what collectively we might do to right [our children's] moral compass."[169] Obama once told an interviewer, "In America we have this strong bias toward individual action. You know, we idolize the John Wayne hero who comes in to correct things with both guns blazing. But individual actions, individual dreams, are not sufficient. We must unite in collective action, build collective institutions and organizations."[170]

This Obama quotation is the anti-Reagan, not only in its embrace of "collective action" over "individual action" but also in its dismissal of the "John Wayne hero"—a man whom Ronald Reagan knew very well and who happened to be an ardent Reagan political supporter. Reagan himself was a rancher, horseman, and cowboy at heart and in practice (at his actual ranch, not just in movies), and he had a robust faith in the hero who comes in on a white horse and saves the day, the good guy who defeats the bad guy.[171] He had played that role not only in movies but also in real life, first as a lifeguard rescuing people in Dixon, Illinois, and then (as he intended) as a president rescuing America from the malaise of the 1970s and the world from the scourge of atheistic Soviet communism.

Ronald Reagan harbored no bias against individual action at all. From the moment that the Pilgrims arrived on America's shores, this was a country where individuals had the faith and freedom to aspire to whatever they wanted. America, Reagan insisted, was a country filled with individual heroes. It had always been. Here was the one place on earth—the last best hope on earth—where an immigrant could walk off a ship at Ellis Island with no money and lots of hope and achieve the American dream.

To that end, this was one reason why Reagan was no foe of immigration, even going so far as to sign legislation (in 1986) granting amnesty to millions of illegal aliens. As noted by Reagan speechwriter Peter Robinson, instead of denouncing these individuals as undocumented and unwanted, Reagan invited them to become citizens. At the same time, the Immigration Reform and Control Act that Reagan signed into law in 1986 also included aggressive provisions to end illegal immigration, including a 50 percent boost in border guards and penalties for hiring undocumented workers. "The amnesty dealt with illegals who were already here," explains Ed Meese, who was Reagan's attorney general at the time. "The rest of the '86 act was intended to get control of the problem so we didn't have any more coming in."[172]

Still, Reagan's heart was open to these individuals, just as he felt America should be open to them. Or, to paraphrase his Farewell Address, if the Shining City had walls, "the walls had doors and the doors were open to anyone with the will and the heart to get here." That was how Reagan saw it.

A decade earlier, in a 1977 radio talk, Reagan had dismissed "the illegal alien fuss," insisting on the benefits of immigrant labor. In a "hungry world," said Reagan, "no regulation or law should be allowed if it results in crops rotting in the field for lack of harvesters."[173]

As a Californian, and California governor, Reagan saw up close the value of immigrant workers. They came to America to strive and fight for a better life, as had the Irish immigrants of Reagan's own family a century earlier. These new Americans were the backbone of the country, taking on the tough jobs that natives refused, epitomizing the nation's work ethic and the promise of the American dream. They were hardworking individuals worthy of respect and access to the dream.

There are many ways to demonstrate Ronald Reagan's respect for the individual, but here are just a few added examples.

On a cold evening in Dixon, Illinois in the early 1930s, a young Ronald "Dutch" Reagan brought home two African-American football players who were teammates. The boys had been denied access to a local hotel, rejected because of the color of their skin. Reagan assured them they would be welcomed at his home, and they were. "Come in, boys," said his mother, Nelle, with a warm smile. They spent the night.[174]

Ronald Reagan had learned racial, ethnic, and religious tolerance from his parents. It had been part of him since his early childhood. He abhorred racism, an aspect of his character both unmistakably clear and not widely appreciated.[175] "I've lived a long time," he told the National Council of Negro Women in July 1983, "but I can't remember a time in my life when I didn't believe that prejudice and bigotry were the worst of sins."[176]

Obviously, this anecdote about the two young black men, of which many more could be given from Reagan's rich life and experiences, reflects Reagan's hatred of racism, but it also underscores his respect for the inherent human dignity of all people, regardless of their skin color, their ethnic background, or their religious beliefs. For Reagan, these were simple, black-and-white matters of basic human worth. All individuals merited our common decency.

To that end, and as a final example of Reagan's respect for the individual, a series of more philosophical statements demonstrates that respect in a way that unifies elements highlighted throughout this book. They occurred in a very hot year in the Reagan presidency and the Cold War: 1983.

That year, in February, Reagan issued a formal proclamation declaring 1983 the Year of the Bible. In doing so, he endured heaps of ridicule from the secular liberal elite. More positively, however, he had seized another teachable moment, publicly underscoring the God-given inalienable rights of the individual.[177] These were rights, Reagan had often said, granted "by the grace of God," and thus, "no government on earth can take them from you."[178] Reagan had enormous admiration for the Declaration of Independence, borrowing its language unremittingly in speeches throughout his life. One of his stronger such presidential statements came in March 1983—again, the Evil Empire speech:

> The basis of those ideals and principles is a commitment to freedom and personal liberty that, itself, is grounded in the much deeper realization that freedom prospers only where the blessings of God are avidly sought and humbly accepted.
> The American experiment in democracy rests on this insight. Its discovery was the great triumph of our Founding Fathers, voiced by William Penn when he said: "If we will not be governed by God, we must be governed by tyrants." Explaining the inalienable rights of men, Jefferson said, "The God who gave us life, gave us liberty at the same time." The evidence of this permeates our history and our government. The Declaration of Independence mentions the Supreme Being no less than four times.[179]

From Washington to Beijing to Moscow, Reagan repeatedly touted the three inalienable rights cited by Thomas Jefferson: life, liberty, and the pursuit of happiness. An inalienable right is one that all individuals are born with, that is inherent to one's being, that cannot be separated from a person; in Jefferson's famous phrase, these rights were endowed in every human by the Creator. Reagan claimed that this "explicit promise" in the Declaration—that all of us are endowed with inalienable rights—is in fact "a principle for eternity, America's deepest treasure."

In an August 1983 address in Atlanta, Reagan shared this particular thought. He quoted a theologian who said that these rights are "corollaries of the great proposition, at the heart of Western civilization, that every . . . person is a *ressacra*, a sacred reality, and as such is entitled to the opportunity of fulfilling those great human potentials with which God has endowed man."[180]

This is worth our pondering, especially in understanding Reagan conservatism and its championing of the individual person. To repeat, Reagan considered every person to be a *sacred* reality. This, Reagan believed, was an *eternal* principle. Combining this Reagan belief with Reagan's belief that human life begins at conception makes his assertion all the more powerful.

At the level of foreign policy, it was obvious to Reagan that when communists unjustly killed their own citizens, they violated God's inalienable right to life. Reagan took it further, seeing communists' seizure or infringement on individual liberty and property as added violations of God's inherent rights to all individuals. To Reagan, the most basic, proper function of government was to protect life, liberty, and property. And there was no greater intrusion than a government effort to suppress or try to control one's freedom to worship God. This violation was an attempt to contain the soul itself—the eternal soul gifted to each and every individual.

Here, too, Soviet communism offered Reagan a crucial point of contrast. It presented him with another valuable civics lesson, if not moral lesson. Reagan provided just that in a bold July 1983 speech, where he laid out what he categorized as the two basic "visions of the world":

> Two visions of the world remain locked in dispute. The first believes all men are created equal by a loving God who has blessed us with freedom. Abraham Lincoln spoke for us ...

The second vision believes that religion is opium for the masses. It believes that eternal principles like truth, liberty, and democracy have no meaning beyond the whim of the state. And Lenin spoke for them.[181]

In Reagan's view, the American Founders had anchored their experiment in absolute truth; the Bolsheviks deliberately established an antithetical model. Reagan said of the Bolshevik Revolution, "only one so-called revolution puts itself above God."[182] The Bolshevik Revolution was a uniquely hellish one. These were disputing visions—inherently in opposition at their very source.

In America, every person was and is a sacred reality. It was a "profound truth," said Reagan, that the "soul," more than the "physical," was "truly important."[183] Because they have eternal souls, individuals are incomparably more important than a temporal state. For a noneternal state to attempt to deny an eternal individual was intolerable and unacceptable.

To Reagan, the individual is always superior to the state; the former is forever, the latter is fleeting. The individual takes form in the womb and remains just as vital throughout all stages of life. No matter what its stage or station, the individual has a sacred dignity that must always be protected and defended.

To a conservative, surely a Reagan conservative, every individual is special, unique, a potential producer with value and new dreams and ideas, one who adds to the world, not subtracts from it; every new individual is not to be lamented as yet another burden on the state, on poverty rolls, on redistribution, on "over-population," on the environment's precious "limited" resources, as another mouth the government must feed. Every new individual, beginning in the womb, holds promise and is to be welcomed, not feared, shunned, and certainly not destroyed.

A New Time for Choosing

In all, this is what Ronald Reagan believed. These "Reagan 11" comprise the essence of Reagan's conservative philosophy—of Reagan conservatism. Much more could be said, from extended analysis of Reagan's statements on the family to his warnings about excessive government regulation of business. Nonetheless, these 11 get at the real Reagan, helping to provide some contours to the mantle that so many Republicans today want to claim.

So, when hearing a Republican presidential aspirant invoking the name of Ronald Reagan, consider whether the candidate shares Reagan's faith-based optimism, his belief in the individual, his belief in American exceptionalism, his regard for the sanctity and dignity of unborn human life. Is the candidate the pessimist in the room full of toys or the optimist searching for the pony in the dung heap? Would the candidate submit the "foundational" and "divine institution" of the family to the harm of the latest cultural trend, dictate, fad, or fashion? If you hear a self-professing conservative heralding "freedom," ask whether he or she believes that a self-governing nation can govern freely without the vital moral rudder that is faith. Can there be genuine freedom without faith? What did Tocqueville say? Reagan said what Tocqueville said.

This, and more, is what a Reagan conservative would say.

And finally, Reagan's conservatism was not merely an enunciation of his personal ideology but was also an affirmation of his personal idea of America and what it means to be an American. Reagan said that America is less of a place than an idea. It certainly was in his mind's eye. Understanding Reagan's conservatism also means understanding Reagan's very concept of the idea of America. Really, then, to answer the question "What is a Reagan conservative?" is less a particular political lesson than an enduring civics lesson. It has value for all American citizens going forward.

And speaking of going forward, it is a lesson that should have special resonance for conservative Republicans who, like Ronald Reagan, want to take their party in a conservative direction as they endeavor to recapture the White House and re-change the nation. In his ongoing messages to his fellow conservatives at CPAC, Reagan essentially told them to be not afraid—that is, to be not afraid of conservatism, to not fear who and what they are. "The time has come," he confidently told them in February 1977, four years before his presidency.

What kind of time? Only Reagan the optimist could have been so optimistic. The Republican Party at the time was in a shambles after Watergate, the withdrawal from Vietnam, the uninspiring Ford presidency, Rockefeller Republicanism, détente and accommodation of the Soviets, the Democratic leadership in the White House, and more. Two terms of Republican control of the White House had merely opened the door for Jimmy Carter, who, as Reagan spoke, had been sworn in just two weeks earlier.

What time had come?

Reagan had a decade earlier called it a "Time for Choosing." A time, he dramatically said, to preserve for America's children "this, the last best hope of man on earth."[184] Choosing wrong, warned Reagan, meant opting for a long period of "darkness." Reagan believed that conservatism shined a guiding light through the darkness.

So, now it was February 1977, and things seemed dark, grim, but Reagan saw them altogether differently, filtering these mere eyesores through the prism of his characteristic sunny optimism. Now, assured Reagan, it was time at last for principled politics and political principles, for conservatives "to present a program of action," one that did not cast aside social conservatism or economic conservatism. They needed to defend both the family and limited government, faith and freedom, the dignity of the human person, and lower taxes. Each side, the social and economic, was half of a "politically effective" conservative whole that needed to be communicated, needed to be shared, needed to be boldly expressed, needed to be not afraid, so that Americans everywhere understood that conservatism provided their natural political home. Despite the considerable political setbacks they faced, conservatives should not be downcast. "We can do it in America," Reagan insisted. "This is not a dream, a wistful hope. It is and has been a reality. I have seen the conservative future and it works."

Now *that* is Reagan conservatism.

Select
Reagan Speeches

Remarks to the Fourth Annual Conservative Political Action Conference (CPAC)
— February 6, 1977 —

This is the text of Ronald Reagan's speech to the fourth annual Conservative Political Action Conference in Washington, DC. Reagan was a regular at CPAC before it was the CPAC we know today—a mass gathering of multiple thousands of conservative faithful and every conceivable major name in the conservative movement and Republican Party. This was Reagan's third CPAC speech, given, incidentally, on his sixty-sixth birthday. By the end of his presidency a decade later, Reagan had addressed CPAC twelve times. In this lengthy 5,300-word speech (this version is excerpted), Reagan explains what it means to be a conservative and urges conservatives not to leave the Republican Party but to work within the GOP (what Reagan called a New Republican Party) as a means to get elected and change America in a conservative direction.

I'm happy to be back with you in this annual event after missing last year's meeting. I had some business in New Hampshire that wouldn't wait.

Three weeks ago here in our nation's capital I told a group of conservative scholars that we are currently in the midst of a re-ordering of the political realities that have shaped our time. We know today that the principles and values that lie at the heart of conservatism are shared by the majority.

Despite what some in the press may say, we who are proud to call ourselves "conservative" are not a minority of a minority party; we are part of the great majority of Americans of both major parties and of most of the independents as well.

A Harris poll released September 7, 1975, showed 18 percent identifying themselves as liberal and 31 percent as conservative, with 41 percent as middle of the road; a few months later, on January 5, 1976, by a 43–19 plurality, those polled by Harris said they would "prefer to see the country move in a more conservative direction than a liberal one."

Last October 24th, the Gallup organization released the result of a poll taken right in the midst of the presidential campaign.

Respondents were asked to state where they would place themselves on a scale ranging from "right-of-center" (which was defined as "conservative") to left-of-center (which was defined as "liberal").

- *Thirty-seven percent viewed themselves as left-of-center or liberal.*
- *Twelve percent placed themselves in the middle.*
- *Fifty-one percent said they were right-of-center, that is, conservative.*

What I find interesting about this particular poll is that it offered those polled a range of choices on a left-right continuum. This seems to me to be a more realistic approach than dividing the world into strict left and rights. Most of us, I guess, like to think of ourselves as avoiding both extremes, and the fact that a majority of Americans chose one or the other position on the right end of the spectrum is really impressive.

Those polls confirm that most Americans are basically conservative in their outlook. But once we have said this, we conservatives have not solved our problems, we have merely stated them clearly. Yes, conservatism can and does mean different things to those who call themselves conservatives.

You know, as I do, that most commentators make a distinction between [what] they call "social" conservatism and "economic" conservatism. The so-called social issues—law and order, abortion, busing, quota systems—are usually associated with blue-collar, ethnic and religious groups themselves traditionally associated with the Democratic Party. The economic issues—inflation, deficit spending and big government—are usually associated with Republican Party members and independents who concentrate their attention on economic matters.

Now I am willing to accept this view of two major kinds of conservatism—or, better still, two different conservative constituencies. But at the same time let me say that the old lines that once clearly divided these two kinds of conservatism are disappearing.

In fact, the time has come to see if it is possible to present a program of action based on political principle that can attract those interested in the so-called "social" issues and those interested in "economic" issues. In short, isn't it possible to combine the two major segments of contemporary American conservatism into one politically effective whole?

I believe the answer is: Yes, it is possible to create a political entity that will reflect the views of the great, hitherto [unacknowledged], conservative majority. We went a long way toward doing it in California. We can do it in America. This is not a dream, a wistful hope. It is and has been a reality. I have seen the conservative future and it works.

Let me say again what I said to our conservative friends from the academic world: What I envision is not simply a melding together of the two branches of American conservatism into a temporary uneasy alliance, but the creation of a new, lasting majority.

This will mean compromise. But not a compromise of basic principle. What will emerge will be something new: something open and vital and dynamic, something the great conservative majority will recognize as its own, because at the heart of this undertaking is principled politics.

I have always been puzzled by the inability of some political and media types to understand exactly what is meant by adherence to political principle. All too often in the press and the television evening news it is treated as a call for "ideological purity." Whatever ideology may mean—and it seems to mean a variety of things, depending upon who is using it—it always conjures up in my mind a picture of a rigid, irrational clinging to abstract theory in the face of reality. We have to recognize that in this country "ideology" is a scare word. And for good reason. Marxist-Leninism is, to give but one example, an ideology. All the facts of the real world have to be fitted to the Procrustean bed of Marx and Lenin. If the facts don't happen to fit the ideology, the facts are chopped off and discarded.

I consider this to be the complete opposite to principled conservatism. If there is any political viewpoint in this world which is free from slavish adherence to abstraction, it is American conservatism.

When a conservative states that the free market is the best mechanism ever devised by the mind of man to meet material needs, he is merely stating what a careful examination of the real world has told him is the truth.

When a conservative says that totalitarian Communism is an absolute enemy of human freedom he is not theorizing—he is reporting the ugly reality captured so unforgettably in the writings of Alexander Solzhenitsyn.

When a conservative says it is bad for the government to spend more than it takes in, he is simply showing the same common sense that tells him to come in out of the rain.

When a conservative says that busing does not work, he is not appealing to some theory of education—he is merely reporting what he has seen down at the local school.

When a conservative quotes Jefferson that government that is closest to the people is best, it is because he knows that Jefferson risked his life, his fortune and his sacred honor to make certain that what he and his fellow patriots learned from experience was not crushed by an ideology of empire.

Conservatism is the antithesis of the kind of ideological fanaticism that has brought so much horror and destruction to the world.

The common sense and common decency of ordinary men and women, working out their own lives in their own way—this is the heart of American conservatism today. Conservative wisdom and principles are derived from willingness to learn, not just from what is going on now, but from what has happened before.

The principles of conservatism are sound because they are based on what men and women have discovered through experience in not just one generation or a dozen, but in all the combined experience of mankind. When we conservatives say that we know something about political affairs, and that we know can be stated as principles, we are saying that the principles we hold dear are those that have been found, through experience, to be ultimately beneficial for individuals, for families, for communities and for nations—found through the often bitter testing of pain, or sacrifice and sorrow.

One thing that must be made clear in post-Watergate is this: The American new conservative majority we represent is not based on abstract theorizing of the kind that turns off the American people, but on common sense, intelligence, reason, hard work, faith in God, and the guts to say: "Yes, there are things we do strongly believe in, that we are willing to live for, and yes, if necessary, to die for." That is not "ideological purity." It is simply what built this country and kept it great.

Let us lay to rest, once and for all, the myth of a small group of ideological purists trying to capture a majority. Replace it with the reality of a majority trying to assert its rights against the tyranny of powerful academics, fashionable left-revolutionaries, some economic illiterates who happen to hold elective office and the social engineers who dominate the dialogue and set the format in political and social affairs. If there is any ideological fanaticism in American political life, it is to be found among the enemies of freedom on the left or right—those who would sacrifice principle to theory, those who worship only the god of political, social and economic abstractions, ignoring the realities of everyday life. They are not conservatives.

Our first job is to get this message across to those who share most of our principles. If we allow ourselves to be portrayed as ideological shock troops without correcting this error we are doing ourselves and our cause a disservice. Wherever and whenever we can, we should gently but firmly correct our political and media friends who have been perpetuating the myth of conservatism as a narrow ideology. Whatever the word may have meant in the past, today conservatism means principles evolving from experience and a belief in change when necessary, but not just for the sake of change.

Once we have established this, the next question is: What will be the political vehicle by which the majority can assert its rights?

I have to say I cannot agree with some of my friends—perhaps including some of you here tonight—who have answered that question by saying this nation needs a new political party.

I respect that view and I know that those who have reached it have done so after long hours of study. But I believe that political success of the principles we believe in can best be achieved in the Republican Party. I believe the Republican Party can hold and should provide the political mechanism through which the goals of the majority of Americans can be achieved. For one thing, the biggest single grouping of conservatives is to be found in that party. It makes more sense to build on that grouping than to break it up and start over. Rather than a third party, we can have a new first party made up of people who share our principles. [. . .]

Our candidates must be willing to communicate with every level of society, because the principles we espouse are universal and cut across traditional lines. In every Congressional district there should be a search made for young men and women who share these principles and they should be brought into positions of leadership in the local Republican Party groups. We can find attractive, articulate candidates if we look, and when we find them, we will begin to change the sorry state of affairs that has led to a Democratic-controlled

Congress for more than 40 years. I need not remind you that you can have the soundest principles in the world, but if you don't have candidates who can communicate those principles, candidates who are articulate as well as principled, you are going to lose election after election. I refuse to believe that the good Lord divided this world into Republicans who defend basic values and Democrats who win elections. We have to find tough, bright young men and women who are sick and tired of clichés and the pomposity and the mind-numbing economic idiocy of the liberals in Washington. [. . .]

We believe that liberty can be measured by how much freedom Americans have to make their own decisions, even their own mistakes. Government must step in when one's liberties impinge on one's neighbor's. Government must protect constitutional rights, deal with other governments, protect citizens from aggressors, assure equal opportunity, and be compassionate in caring for those citizens who are unable to care for themselves.

Our federal system of local-state-national government is designed to sort out on what level these actions should be taken. Those concerns of a national character—such as air and water pollution that do not respect state boundaries, or the national transportation system, or efforts to safeguard your civil liberties— must, of course, be handled on the national level.

As a general rule, however, we believe that government action should be taken first by the government that resides as close to you as possible.

We also believe that Americans, often acting through voluntary organizations, should have the opportunity to solve many of the social problems of their communities. This spirit of freely helping others is uniquely American and should be encouraged in every way by government.

Families must continue to be the foundation of our nation.

Families—not government programs—are the best way to make sure our children are properly nurtured, our elderly are cared for, our cultural and spiritual heritages are perpetuated, our laws are observed, and our values are preserved.

Thus it is imperative that our government's programs, actions, officials, and social welfare institutions never be allowed to jeopardize the family. We fear the government may be powerful enough to destroy our families; we know that it is not powerful enough to replace them. [. . .]

Every dollar spent by government is a dollar earned by individuals. Government must always ask: Are your dollars being wisely spent? Can we afford it? Is it not better for the country to leave your dollars in your pocket?

Elected officials, their appointees, and government workers are expected to perform their public acts with honesty, openness, diligence, and special integrity.

Government must work for the goal of justice and the elimination of unfair practices, but no government has yet designed a more productive economic system or one which benefits as many people as the American market system.

The beauty of our land is our legacy to our children. It must be protected by us so that they can pass it on intact to their children.

The United States must always stand for peace and liberty in the world and the rights of the individual. We must form sturdy partnerships with our allies for the preservation of freedom. We must be ever willing to negotiate differences, but equally mindful that there are American ideals that cannot be compromised. Given that there are other nations with potentially hostile design, we recognize that we can reach our goals only while maintaining a superior national defense, second to none.

In his inaugural speech President Carter said that he saw the world "dominated by a new spirit." He said, and I quote: "The passion for freedom is on the rise."

Well, I don't know how he knows this, but if it is true, then it is the most unrequited passion in human history. The world is being dominated by a new spirit, all right, but it isn't the spirit of freedom.

It isn't very often you see a familiar object that shocks and frightens you. But the other day I came across a map of the world created by Freedom House, an organization monitoring the state of freedom in the world for the past 25 years. It is an ordinary map, with one exception: it shows the world's nations in white for free, shaded for partly free and black for not free.

Almost all of the great Eurasian land mass is completely colored black, from the western border of East Germany, through middle and eastern Europe, through the awesome spaces of the Soviet Union, on to the Bering Strait in the north, down past the immensity of China, still further down to Vietnam and the South China Sea—in all that huge, sprawling, inconceivably immense area not a single political or personal or religious freedom exists. The entire continent of Africa, from the Mediterranean to the Cape of Good Hope, from the Atlantic to the Indian Ocean, all that vastness is almost totally unfree. In the tiny nation of Tanzania alone, according to a report in the *New York Times*, there are 3,000 people in detention for political crimes—that is more than the total being held in South Africa! The Mideast has only one free state: Israel. If a visitor from another planet were to approach earth, and if this planet showed free nations in light and unfree nations in darkness, the pitifully small beacons of light would make him wonder what was hidden in that terrifying, enormous blackness.

We know what is hidden: Gulag. Torture. Families—and human beings—broken apart. No free press, no freedom of religion. The ancient forms of tyranny revived and made even more hideous and strong through what Winston Churchill once called "a perverted science." Men rotting for years in solitary confinement because they have different political and economic beliefs, solitary confinement that drives the fortunate ones insane and makes the survivors wish for death.

Only now and then do we in the West hear a voice from out of that darkness. Then there is silence—the silence of human slavery.

There is no more terrifying sound in human experience, with one possible exception. Look at that map again. The very heart of the darkness is the Soviet Union and from that heart comes a different sound. It is the whirring sound of machinery and the whisper of the computer technology we ourselves have sold them. It is the sound of building, building of the strongest military machine ever devised by man. Our military strategy is designed to hopefully prevent a war. Theirs is designed to win one. A group of eminent scientists, scholars and intelligence experts offer a survey showing that the Soviet Union is driving for military superiority and are derided as hysterically making, quote, "a worst case," unquote, concerning Soviet intentions and capabilities.

But is it not precisely the duty of the national government to be prepared for the worst case? [. . .]

We don't want hysteria. We don't want distortion of Soviet power. We want truth. And above all we want peace. And to have [recognition] that the United States has to immediately re-examine its entire view of the world and develop a strategy of freedom. We cannot be the second-best super-power for the simple reason that he who is second is last. In this deadly game, there are no silver medals for second. [. . .]

We can never go wrong if we do what is morally right. [. . .]

There is only one major question on the agenda of national priorities and that is the state of our national security. I refer, of course, to the state of our armed forces—but also to our state of mind, to the way we perceive the world. We cannot maintain the strength we need to survive, no matter how many missiles we have, no matter how many tanks we build, unless we are willing to reverse:

- The trend of deteriorating faith in and continuing abuse of our national intelligence agencies. Let's stop the sniping and the propaganda and the historical revisionism and let the CIA and the other intelligence agencies do their job!

- Let us reverse the trend of public indifference to problems of national security. In every congressional district citizens should join together, enlist, and educate neighbors and make certain that congressmen know we care. The front pages of major newspapers on the East Coast recently headlined and told in great detail of a takeover, the takeover of a magazine published in New York—not a nation losing its freedom. You would think, from the attention it received in the media, that it was a matter of blazing national interest whether the magazine lived or died. The tendency of much of the media to ignore the state of our national security is too well documented for me to go on.

My friends, the time has come to start acting to bring about the great conservative majority party we know is waiting to be created.

And just to set the record straight, let me say this about our friends who are now Republicans but who do not identify themselves as conservatives: I want the record to show that I do not view the new revitalized Republican Party as one based on a principle of exclusion. After all, you do not get to be a majority party by searching for groups you won't associate or work with. If we truly believe in our principles, we should sit down and talk. Talk with anyone, anywhere, at any time if it means talking about the principles for the Republican Party. Conservatism is not a narrow ideology, nor is it the exclusive property of conservative activists.

We've succeeded better than we know. Little more than a decade ago more than two-thirds of Americans believed the federal government could solve all our problems, and do so without restricting our freedom or bankrupting the nation.

We warned of things to come, of the danger inherent in unwarranted government involvement in things not its proper province. What we warned against has come to pass. And today more than two-thirds of our citizens are telling us, and each other, that social engineering by the federal government has failed. The

Great Society is great only in power, in size and in cost. And so are the problems it set out to solve. Freedom has been diminished and we stand on the brink of economic ruin.

Our task now is not to sell a philosophy, but to make the majority of Americans, who already share that philosophy, see that modern conservatism offers them a political home. We are not a cult, we are members of a majority. Let's act and talk like it.

The job is ours and the job must be done. If not by us, who? If not now, when?

Our party must be the party of the individual. It must not sell out the individual to cater to the group. No greater challenge faces our society today than ensuring that each one of us can maintain his dignity and his identity in an increasingly complex, centralized society.

Extreme taxation, excessive controls, oppressive government competition with business, galloping inflation, frustrated minorities and forgotten Americans are not the products of free enterprise. They are the residue of centralized bureaucracy, of government by a self-anointed elite.

Our party must be based on the kind of leadership that grows and takes its strength from the people. Any organization is in actuality only the lengthened shadow of its members. A political party is a mechanical structure created to further a cause. The cause, not the mechanism, brings and holds the members together. And our cause must be to rediscover, reassert and reapply America's spiritual heritage to our national affairs.

Then with God's help we shall indeed be as a city upon a hill with the eyes of all people upon us.

Address at the Bicentennial of Georgetown University
— October 1, 1988 —

At Georgetown University on October 1, 1988, Ronald Reagan gave one of his best, most philosophical, and yet neglected orations of his presidency. It was a statement about America, about educating, and about educating Americans in American ideals and principles. It was also a significant testimony not only to Reagan's belief in the "twin beacons" of faith and freedom but also to the vital importance of Americans not separating faith and freedom from education, and particularly higher education. A truly worthwhile education was, in Reagan's mind, one that understood the reinforcing relationship between faith and freedom. Reagan also believed that understanding conservatism—that is, educating oneself in conservatism—was about understanding this relationship.

Thank you, Father [Timothy S.] Healy, Father [J. Donald] Freeze, and [former U.S. ambassador] Jeane Kirkpatrick, and thank you all very much. It is indeed a great privilege in these, the closing days of my service in Washington, to receive an honor such as this and a welcome such as the one that you've just given me.

It puts me in mind of a story about a remarkable man—a classic scholar, a scientist, a humanitarian—who once received an honorary degree from a great institution of higher learning. And the fellow introducing him said, "We are about to hear from a great man, a noble man, a man of courage, a man of honor, yes, a man to whom the entire world owes a debt of gratitude." And the man rose from his chair and took the podium, as I just did, and the crowd cheered. And he looked out at the audience, and then he turned back to the other fellow and said, "How come you didn't tell them about how humble and modest I am?" [Laughter]

Well, unlike him—[laughter]—the greeting you've just given me really does make me feel modest and humble, and so does the degree you've bestowed upon me today. It certainly would have pleased my blessed mother. She always wanted me to be a doctor. [Laughter] But it also means a great deal to me.

We're celebrating the bicentennial of Georgetown University. I have a great affection for Georgetown. After all, it's one of the few things in this country that are older than I am. [Laughter] In the year that Georgetown first came to be, the political system designed by our Constitution was inaugurated as well, and our first President was chosen. Georgetown is the oldest Catholic university in this country. And the political system of the United States has been the world's most stable over the course of the past two centuries. But only in the eyes of men are they old. In the eyes of God, these past two centuries have been but the briefest moment in the onrush of time whose meaning is truly known to Him alone. I would hope that He would be pleased with America and Georgetown, and would view both with the special fondness and, perhaps, the occasional exasperation that any precocious child invokes in his father.

For the truth is, both Georgetown and these United States are in their infancy, experiments that test what is best and noblest in us. There was reason to imagine that the American experiment could not last; and that there were moments when men of good will thought the experiment was doomed, as during those tragic Civil War years, when American fought against American and tore this country asunder so that it could be reassembled as a freer and better place. There have been other experiments as well during these centuries— terrible, awful experiments that demonstrate just how unyielding is God's commitment to the covenant he made with Abraham. For there must have been times, in the showers of Treblinka or on the killing fields of Cambodia or in the forests of Katyn, when men and women in their anguish and despair must have expected that the great flood would once again sweep away the sinning nations. Or they might have been seized with the same sentiment as the poet Yeats when haunted by the sight of a world in which "The best lack all conviction, while the worst are full of passionate intensity." "Surely," Yeats wrote, "some revolution—revelation," I should say, "is at hand; surely the Second Coming is at hand."

Well, yesterday we commemorated a dark day in the course of our century: the fiftieth anniversary of the signing of the Munich pact. On this day fifty years ago, Prime Minister Neville Chamberlain returned to Britain and proclaimed that he had brought "peace in our time." And 11 months later, Nazi Germany invaded Poland, hurling that nation into a nightmare from which it has yet to awake and throwing the world into war. And yet, just at the very moments that the worst seemed destined to defeat the best, the best pulled something out of themselves and were not consumed. Three barbaric governments were eliminated, and Germany, Italy, and Japan became inseparable allies to those whom they had fought only a few years before.

And though millions and millions still live under the yoke of communism, they have proved that the human spirit cannot be consumed either. There have been men and women who make us gasp with wonder at the greatness thrust upon them when oppression proved too much to tolerate. I think of the sight of Natan Sharansky still in the dominion of his KGB captors, zigzagging his way across the tarmac after they ordered him to walk a straight line from the plane that had carried him to freedom. It was one of those moments when laughter and tears commingle, and one does not know when the first leaves off and the second begins. It was a vision of the purest freedom known to man, the freedom of a man whose cause is just and whose faith is his guiding light.

At its full flowering, freedom is the first principle of society; this society, Western society. Indeed, from Abraham to Plato, Aristotle to Aquinas, freedom is the animating principle of Western civilization. Freedom comes in many guises: in the noble words of the Declaration of Independence and in the noble souls of people like Sharansky.[185] And yet freedom cannot exist alone. And that's why the theme for your bicentennial is so very apt: learning, faith, and freedom. Each reinforces the others, each makes the others possible. For what are they without each other?

Learning is a good thing, but unless it's tempered by faith and a love of freedom, it can be very dangerous indeed. The names of many intellectuals are recorded on the rolls of infamy, from Robespierre to Lenin to Ho Chi Minh to Pol Pot. We must never forget that wisdom is impossible without learning, but learning does not—not by the longest measure—bring wisdom. It can also bring evil. What will faith without a respect for learning and an understanding of freedom bring? We've seen the tragedy of untempered faith in the hellish deaths of 14-year-old boys—small hands still wrapped around machine guns—on the front lines in Iran.

And what will be wrought by freedom unaccompanied by learning and faith?—the license of Weimar Germany and the decadence of imperial Rome; human behavior untempered by a sense of moral, spiritual, or intellectual limits—the behavior G. K. Chesterton described as the "morbid weakness of always sacrificing the normal to the abnormal." And when freedom is mangled in this way, what George Orwell would have called unfreedom soon follows.

So, we like to believe, and we pray it will always be so, that America is different, that America is what she is because she is guided by all three: learning, faith, and freedom. Our love of knowledge has made this nation the intellectual and technological center of the world. Our commitment to protecting and preserving the freedoms we enjoy is unshakable. And our faith is what supports us. Tocqueville said it in 1835, and it's as true today as it was then: "Despotism may govern without faith, but liberty cannot. Religion is more needed in democratic societies than in any others."

Americans know the truth of those words. We still believe in our Creator. We still believe in knowledge. We still believe in freedom. We're committed to providing the world with the bounties we enjoy, and we're sickened by those societies that do dishonor to humankind by denying human beings their birthright. We grieve for the millions who have perished even in this decade because their freedoms were denied, and we must not dishonor them by allowing those who follow us on this Earth to say those millions died for nothing, that we lived in an age of barbarism.

No, ladies and gentlemen, I believe that if we hold fast and true to our principles our time will come to be known as the age of freedom. There are signs—and they're only signs—that suggest the rulers who enslave and victimize the people of the Earth are on the ideological defensive. Their claims for the superiority of failed and terrible philosophies are sounding ever more hollow. The societies they designed to be utopias have not, to put it mildly, turned out as planned. To save themselves, those rulers are beginning to cast their eyes toward the democratic societies they used to revile. There are signs, only signs, that these rulers are beginning to understand the secret to our prosperity: We prosper economically only because people are free, free not only to speak and read and think but also to create and build and barter and sell.

Now, we're fast approaching a turning point in the history of this age. It'll determine whether history will deem our time the age of freedom or the age of barbarism. We have been steadfast and unapologetic about our defense of our beliefs and our defense of our societies. We learned the lesson of Munich. When we were told that the time had come to accept Soviet nuclear superiority in Europe, we said we would never accept it; when we were told that the time had come to accept the Soviet dominion over Afghanistan, we said we would never accept it; and when we were told that we had no chance to dislodge Soviet proxies in Angola and Nicaragua, we said we would never accept it.

And you all know what has happened. In the last 8 years, not an inch of ground has fallen to communism. Indeed, we liberated the island of Grenada from the "mere anarchy" it had fallen into under Communist rule, and set it on the road to democracy. And we helped save a country from communism and watched it flower into a democracy in the midst of a civil war: the Nation of El Salvador. Yes, at every point on the map that the Soviets have applied pressure, we've done all we can to apply pressure against them. And now we're seeing a sight many believed they would never see in our lifetime: the receding of the tide of totalitarianism.

Now, I want to tell you all one thing. Contrary to some of the things you've heard, I'm the same man I was when I came to Washington. I believe the same things I believed when I came to Washington. And I think those beliefs have been vindicated by the success of the policies to which we held fast. But now—just at the moment when we're required by history to hold the line, to hold true to our principles, and to apply the lessons of our learning, our faith, and our freedom—some of our most distinguished and thoughtful people have taken a look at the world today and determined that America is in decline.

America in decline? Orwell once said that some ideas were so foolish only intellectuals could believe them. [Laughter] Well, this is perhaps the most foolish idea of the present day. We live in the most prosperous, the freest society the world has ever known; and yet they say we're in decline. We've had almost six years of uninterrupted economic recovery, and yet they say we're in decline.

They say we're in decline because they believe we're spread too thin around the globe, that our military commitments are too vast and too difficult and that we suffer from a condition called overstretch. Overstretch? Well, consider these truths. In 1955 we spent around 11 percent of our gross national product on defense. In 1988, around 6 percent—not quite enough, in my view, but still substantial. Some overstretch! In 1955 we had more than 3 million Americans in uniform. Today we have about 2 million Americans in uniform. Some overstretch!

And despite what you've heard, let the Commander in Chief assure you of one thing: We have not been accumulating nuclear weapons. In fact, the number of weapons in our nuclear stockpile was maybe a third higher 20 years ago. Today our weaponry is leaner, more accurate, and better equipped to keep the peace by keeping us strong. Some overstretch!

I was given the honor of manning the nation's helm these past 8 years, so I think I speak with some authority when I tell you, ladies and gentlemen, that the United States of America is not in decline. No, America is still young, still full of promise, and ready to fulfill that promise. She has not reached her apex. It's sad to say, but the false prophets of decline have needlessly *lost* faith at a moment when they should be *taking* faith. They should be taking faith in the ideas that have led us here: faith in the determination of men to be free and faith in the destiny our Maker has written for us. And, yes, ladies and gentlemen, with all my heart I believe that this is the age of freedom.

I want to thank you all for what you've given me. I want to thank Georgetown University for what she's given all of you. And all I want to say to close is, God bless you all, and may God bless America.

Farewell Address to the Nation
— January 11, 1989 —

Ronald Reagan ended his presidency with a goodbye speech, a Farewell Address, given from the Oval Office on January 11, 1989.

The address was written by Reagan speechwriter Peggy Noonan. As Noonan herself has noted, as have other Reagan speechwriters, many of the fortieth president's speeches were inspired in part from previous remarks Reagan himself had written long ago. That is understandable, as the task of a good speechwriter is to create a text that the speech-giver might have written himself. The Farewell Address is one such speech that is so quintessentially Reagan, a stirring rendition masterfully crafted by the gifted pen of Noonan.

In a roughly 3,300-word speech, the president began speaking at 9:02 p.m. from the Oval Office. The address was broadcast live on nationwide radio and television, watched by tens of millions of Americans.[186] Reagan began by informing his "fellow Americans" that this was the thirty-fourth time he had spoken to them from the Oval Office—a very high number for any president—and would also be the last. Soon it would be "time for me to go." But first, however, he "wanted to share some thoughts, some of which I've been saving for a long time." Unbeknownst to most viewers, Reagan had been sharing some of these thoughts for a long time.

It was an exceptional speech about an exceptional America—a Shining City, wind-swept, God-blessed, and what Reagan saw as the world's "last best hope." It was really the perfect image for Reagan to end his presidency and his political career. It pointed to cherished beliefs he held for decades, and a view of America, and its exceptionalism, that he believed had prevailed not only for decades but for centuries.

M y fellow Americans:
       This is the 34th time I'll speak to you from the Oval Office and the last. We've been together eight years now, and soon it'll be time for me to go. But before I do, I wanted to share some thoughts, some of which I've been saving for a long time.

It's been the honor of my life to be your president. So many of you have written the past few weeks to say thanks, but I could say as much to you. Nancy and I are grateful for the opportunity you gave us to serve.

One of the things about the Presidency is that you're always somewhat apart. You spend a lot of time going by too fast in a car someone else is driving, and seeing the people through tinted glass—the parents holding up a child, and the wave you saw too late and couldn't return. And so many times I wanted to stop and reach out from behind the glass, and connect. Well, maybe I can do a little of that tonight.

People ask how I feel about leaving. And the fact is, "parting is such sweet sorrow." The sweet part is California and the ranch and freedom. The sorrow—the goodbyes, of course, and leaving this beautiful place.

You know, down the hall and up the stairs from this office is the part of the White House where the president and his family live. There are a few favorite windows I have up there that I like to stand and look out of early in the morning. The view is over the grounds here to the Washington Monument, and then the Mall and the Jefferson Memorial. But on mornings when the humidity is low, you can see past the Jefferson to the river, the Potomac, and the Virginia shore. Someone said that's the view Lincoln had when he saw the smoke rising from the Battle of Bull Run. I see more prosaic things: the grass on the banks, the morning traffic as people make their way to work, now and then a sailboat on the river.

I've been thinking a bit at that window. I've been reflecting on what the past eight years have meant and mean. And the image that comes to mind like a refrain is a nautical one—a small story about a big ship, and a refugee, and a sailor. It was back in the early eighties, at the height of the boat people. And the sailor was hard at work on the carrier *Midway*, which was patrolling the South China Sea. The sailor, like most American servicemen, was young, smart, and fiercely observant. The crew spied on the horizon a leaky little boat. And crammed inside were refugees from Indochina hoping to get to America. The *Midway* sent a small launch to bring them to the ship and safety. As the refugees made their way through the choppy seas, one spied the sailor on deck, and stood up, and called out to him. He yelled, "Hello, American sailor. Hello, freedom man."

A small moment with a big meaning, a moment the sailor, who wrote it in a letter, couldn't get out of his mind. And, when I saw it, neither could I. Because that's what it was to be an American in the 1980s. We stood, again, for freedom. I know we always have, but in the past few years the world again—and in a way, we ourselves—rediscovered it.

It's been quite a journey this decade, and we held together through some stormy seas. And at the end, together, we are reaching our destination.

The fact is, from Grenada to the Washington and Moscow summits, from the recession of '81 to '82, to the expansion that began in late '82 and continues to this day, we've made a difference. The way I see it, there were two great triumphs, two things that I'm proudest of. One is the economic recovery, in which the people of America created—and filled—19 million new jobs. The other is the recovery of our morale. America is respected again in the world and looked to for leadership.

Something that happened to me a few years ago reflects some of this. It was back in 1981, and I was attending my first big economic summit, which was held that year in Canada. The meeting place rotates among the member countries. The opening meeting was a formal dinner for the heads of government of the seven industrialized nations. Now, I sat there like the new kid in school and listened, and it was all Francois this and Helmut that. They dropped titles and spoke to one another on a first-name basis. Well, at one point I sort of leaned in and said, "My name's Ron." Well, in that same year, we began the actions we felt would ignite an economic comeback—cut taxes and regulation, started to cut spending. And soon the recovery began.

Two years later, another economic summit with pretty much the same cast. At the big opening meeting we all got together, and all of a sudden, just for a moment, I saw that everyone was just sitting there looking at me. And then one of them broke the silence. "Tell us about the American miracle," he said.

Well, back in 1980, when I was running for president, it was all so different. Some pundits said our programs would result in catastrophe. Our views on foreign affairs would cause war. Our plans for the economy would cause inflation to soar and bring about economic collapse. I even remember one highly respected economist saying, back in 1982, that "The engines of economic growth have shut down here, and they're likely to stay that way for years to come." Well, he and the other opinion leaders were wrong. The fact is, what they called "radical" was really "right." What they called "dangerous" was just "desperately needed."

And in all of that time I won a nickname, "The Great Communicator." But I never thought it was my style or the words I used that made a difference: it was the content. I wasn't a great communicator, but I communicated great things, and they didn't spring full bloom from my brow, they came from the heart of a great nation—from our experience, our wisdom, and our belief in the principles that have guided us for two centuries. They called it the Reagan revolution. Well, I'll accept that, but for me it always seemed more like the great rediscovery, a rediscovery of our values and our common sense.

Common sense told us that when you put a big tax on something, the people will produce less of it. So, we cut the people's tax rates, and the people produced more than ever before. The economy bloomed like a plant that had been cut back and could now grow quicker and stronger. Our economic program brought about the longest peacetime expansion in our history: real family income up, the poverty rate down, entrepreneurship booming, and an explosion in research and new technology. We're exporting more than ever because American industry became more competitive and at the same time, we summoned the national will to knock down protectionist walls abroad instead of erecting them at home.

Common sense also told us that to preserve the peace, we'd have to become strong again after years of weakness and confusion. So, we rebuilt our defenses, and this New Year we toasted the new peacefulness around the globe. Not only have the superpowers actually begun to reduce their stockpiles of nuclear weapons—and hope for even more progress is bright—but the regional conflicts that rack the globe are also beginning to cease. The Persian Gulf is no longer a war zone. The Soviets are leaving Afghanistan. The Vietnamese are preparing to pull out of Cambodia, and an American-mediated accord will soon send 50,000 Cuban troops home from Angola.

The lesson of all this was, of course, that because we're a great nation, our challenges seem complex. It will always be this way. But as long as we remember our first principles and believe in ourselves, the future will always be ours. And something else we learned: Once you begin a great movement, there's no telling where it will end. We meant to change a nation, and instead, we changed a world.

Countries across the globe are turning to free markets and free speech and turning away from the ideologies of the past. For them, the great rediscovery of the 1980s has been that, lo and behold, the moral way of government is the practical way of government: Democracy, the profoundly good, is also the profoundly productive.

When you've got to the point when you can celebrate the anniversaries of your 39th birthday you can sit back sometimes, review your life, and see it flowing before you. For me there was a fork in the river, and it was right in the middle of my life. I never meant to go into politics. It wasn't my intention when I was young. But I was raised to believe you had to pay your way for the blessings bestowed on you. I was happy with my career in the entertainment world, but I ultimately went into politics because I wanted to protect something precious.

Ours was the first revolution in the history of mankind that truly reversed the course of government, and with three little words: "We the People." "We the People" tell the government what to do; it doesn't tell us. "We the People" are the driver; the government is the car. And we decide where it should go, and by what route, and how fast. Almost all the world's constitutions are documents in which governments tell the people what their privileges are. Our Constitution is a document in which "We the People" tell the government what it is allowed to do. "We the People" are free. This belief has been the underlying basis for everything I've tried to do these past eight years.

But back in the 1960s, when I began, it seemed to me that we'd begun reversing the order of things—that through more and more rules and regulations and confiscatory taxes, the government was taking more of our money, more of our options, and more of our freedom. I went into politics in part to put up my hand and say, "Stop." I was a citizen politician, and it seemed the right thing for a citizen to do.

I think we have stopped a lot of what needed stopping. And I hope we have once again reminded people that man is not free unless government is limited. There's a clear cause and effect here that is as neat and predictable as a law of physics: As government expands, liberty contracts.

Nothing is less free than pure communism—and yet we have, the past few years, forged a satisfying new closeness with the Soviet

Union. I've been asked if this isn't a gamble, and my answer is no because we're basing our actions not on words but deeds. The detente of the 1970s was based not on actions but promises. They'd promise to treat their own people and the people of the world better. But the gulag was still the gulag; and the state was still expansionist; and they still waged proxy wars in Africa, Asia, and Latin America.

Well, this time, so far, it's different. President Gorbachev has brought about some internal democratic reforms and begun the withdrawal from Afghanistan. He has also freed prisoners whose names I've given him every time we've met.

But life has a way of reminding you of big things through small incidents. Once, during the heady days of the Moscow summit, Nancy and I decided to break off from the entourage one afternoon to visit the shops on Arbat Street—that's a little street just off Moscow's main shopping area. Even though our visit was a surprise, every Russian there immediately recognized us and called out our names and reached for our hands. We were just about swept away by the warmth. You could almost feel the possibilities in all that joy. But within seconds, a KGB detail pushed their way toward us and began pushing and shoving the people in the crowd. It was an interesting moment. It reminded me that while the man on the street in the Soviet Union yearns for peace, the government is Communist. And those who run it are Communists, and that means we and they view such issues as freedom and human rights very differently.

We must keep up our guard, but we must also continue to work together to lessen and eliminate tension and mistrust. My view is that President Gorbachev is different from previous Soviet leaders. I think he knows some of the things wrong with his society and is trying to fix them. We wish him well. And we'll continue to work to make sure that the Soviet Union that eventually emerges from this process is a less threatening one. What it all boils down to is this: I want the new closeness to continue. And it will, as long as we make it clear that we will continue to act in a certain way as long as they continue to act in a helpful manner. If and when they don't, at first pull your punches. If they persist, pull the plug. It's still trust but verify. It's still play, but cut the cards. It's still watch closely. And don't be afraid to see what you see.

I've been asked if I have any regrets. Well, I do. The deficit is one. I've been talking a great deal about that lately, but tonight isn't for arguments, and I'm going to hold my tongue. But an observation: I've had my share of victories in the Congress, but what few people noticed is that I never won anything you didn't win for me. They never saw my troops, they never saw Reagan's regiments, the American people. You won every battle with every call you made and letter you wrote demanding action. Well, action is still needed. If we're to finish the job, Reagan's regiments will have to become the Bush brigades. Soon he'll be the chief, and he'll need you every bit as much as I did.

Finally, there is a great tradition of warnings in Presidential farewells, and I've got one that's been on my mind for some time. But oddly enough it starts with one of the things I'm proudest of in the past eight years: the resurgence of national pride that I called the new patriotism. This national feeling is good, but it won't count for much, and it won't last unless it's grounded in thoughtfulness and knowledge.

An informed patriotism is what we want. And are we doing a good enough job teaching our children what America is and what she represents in the long history of the world? Those of us who are over 35 or so years of age grew up in a different America. We were taught, very directly, what it means to be an American. And we absorbed, almost in the air, a love of country and an appreciation of its institutions. If you didn't get these things from your family you got them from the neighborhood, from the father down the street who fought in Korea or the family who lost someone at Anzio. Or you could get a sense of patriotism from school. And if all else failed you could get a sense of patriotism from the popular culture. The movies celebrated democratic values and implicitly reinforced the idea that America was special. TV was like that, too, through the mid-sixties.

But now, we're about to enter the nineties, and some things have changed. Younger parents aren't sure that an unambivalent appreciation of America is the right thing to teach modern children. And as for those who create the popular culture, well-grounded patriotism is no longer the style. Our spirit is back, but we haven't reinstitutionalized it. We've got to do a better job of getting across that America is freedom—freedom of speech, freedom of religion, freedom of enterprise. And freedom is special and rare. It's fragile; it needs protection.

So, we've got to teach history based not on what's in fashion but what's important—why the Pilgrims came here, who Jimmy Doolittle was, and what those 30 seconds over Tokyo meant. You know, 4 years ago on the 40th anniversary of D-day, I read a letter from a young woman writing to her late father, who'd fought on Omaha Beach. Her name was Lisa Zanatta Henn, and she said, "we will always remember, we will never forget what the boys of Normandy did." Well, let's help her keep her word. If we forget what we did, we won't know who we are. I'm warning of an eradication of the American memory that could result, ultimately, in an erosion of the American spirit. Let's start with some basics: more attention to American history and a greater emphasis on civic ritual.

And let me offer lesson number one about America: All great change in America begins at the dinner table. So, tomorrow night in the kitchen I hope the talking begins. And children, if your parents haven't been teaching you what it means to be an American, let 'em know and nail 'em on it. That would be a very American thing to do.

And that's about all I have to say tonight, except for one thing. The past few days when I've been at that window upstairs, I've thought a bit of the "shining city upon a hill." The phrase comes from John Winthrop, who wrote it to describe the America he imagined. What he imagined was important because he was an early Pilgrim, an early freedom man. He journeyed here on what today we'd call a little wooden boat; and like the other Pilgrims, he was looking for a home that would be free.

I've spoken of the Shining City all my political life, but I don't know if I ever quite communicated what I saw when I said it. But in my mind it was a tall, proud city built on rocks stronger than oceans, wind-swept, God-blessed, and teeming with people of all kinds living in harmony and peace; a city with free ports that hummed with commerce and creativity. And if there had to be city walls, the walls had doors and the doors were open to anyone with the will and the heart to get here. That's how I saw it, and see it still.

And how stands the city on this winter night? More prosperous, more secure, and happier than it was eight years ago. But more than that: After 200 years, two centuries, she still stands strong and true on the granite ridge, and her glow has held steady no matter what storm. And she's still a beacon, still a magnet for all who must have freedom, for all the pilgrims from all the lost places who are hurtling through the darkness, toward home.

We've done our part. And as I walk off into the city streets, a final word to the men and women of the Reagan revolution, the men and women across America who for eight years did the work that brought America back. My friends: We did it. We weren't just marking time. We made a difference. We made the city stronger, we made the city freer, and we left her in good hands. All in all, not bad, not bad at all.

And so, goodbye, God bless you, and God bless the United States of America.

Address to the National Association of Evangelicals
("Evil Empire" Speech)
— March 8, 1983 —

Today we call it the "Evil Empire" speech. But at the time, and still in the official Public Papers of the Presidents repository today, it carries a much tamer and blander title: "Remarks at the Annual Convention of the National Association of Evangelicals." That was the venue, a convention in Orlando, Florida, at the Citrus Crown Ballroom at the Sheraton Twin Towers Hotel. There, on March 8, 1983, Ronald Reagan delivered one of his most controversial and provocative speeches, referring to the Soviet Union as "the focus of evil in the modern world."

The fortieth president hit the dais at 3:04 p.m. and began speaking to the packed, excited room of Christian faithful—and intensely interested journalists. For a speech remembered for its fire-and-brimstone foreign-policy pronouncements, it did not begin that way. The opening salvo of this 3,877-word anticommunist manifesto was a gentle exhortation about the power of prayer and its essentiality to the presidency. The president then proceeded to address a myriad of domestic and social issues, long before getting to foreign policy and the USSR. Of course, it ended with a quite different exhortation.

The speech was pure Ronald Reagan—from start to finish, from home to abroad, from the American Founders he cited to the Soviet leadership he condemned, from the power of prayer to the wickedness of Soviet repression, from faith to freedom. To read and know and understand the Evil Empire speech is to read and know and understand President Ronald Reagan. With this historic speech, the fortieth president gave the world an incisive look not merely inside the Soviet empire but also inside himself. This was one of Reagan's most interesting and revealing speeches; it told us as much about Ronald Reagan as it did the Soviet Union.

Reverend clergy all, Senator Hawkins, distinguished members of the Florida congressional delegation, and all of you:

I can't tell you how you have warmed my heart with your welcome. I'm delighted to be here today.

Those of you in the National Association of Evangelicals are known for your spiritual and humanitarian work. And I would be especially remiss if I didn't discharge right now one personal debt of gratitude. Thank you for your prayers. Nancy and I have felt their presence many times in many ways. And believe me, for us they've made all the difference.

The other day in the East Room of the White House at a meeting there, someone asked me whether I was aware of all the people out there who were praying for the president. And I had to say, "Yes, I am. I've felt it. I believe in intercessionary prayer." But I couldn't help but say to that questioner after he'd asked the question that—or at least say to them that if sometimes when he was praying he got a busy signal, it was just me in there ahead of him. [Laughter] I think I understand how Abraham Lincoln felt when he said, "I have been driven many times to my knees by the overwhelming conviction that I had nowhere else to go."

From the joy and the good feeling of this conference, I go to a political reception. [Laughter] Now, I don't know why, but that bit of scheduling reminds me of a story—[laughter]—which I'll share with you.

An evangelical minister and a politician arrived at Heaven's gate one day together. And St. Peter, after doing all the necessary formalities, took them in hand to show them where their quarters would be. And he took them to a small, single room with a bed, a chair, and a table and said this was for the clergyman. And the politician was a little worried about what might be in store for him. And he couldn't believe it then when St. Peter stopped in front of a beautiful mansion with lovely grounds, many servants, and told him that these would be his quarters.

And he couldn't help but ask, he said, "But wait, how—there's something wrong—how do I get this mansion while that good and holy man only gets a single room?" And St. Peter said, "You have to understand how things are up here. We've got thousands and thousands of clergy. You're the first politician who ever made it." [Laughter]

But I don't want to contribute to a stereotype. [Laughter] So, I tell you there are a great many God-fearing, dedicated, noble men and women in public life, present company included. And, yes, we need your help to keep us ever mindful of the ideas and the principles that brought us into the public arena in the first place. The basis of those ideals and principles is a commitment to freedom and personal liberty that, itself, is grounded in the much deeper realization that freedom prospers only where the blessings of God are avidly sought and humbly accepted.

The American experiment in democracy rests on this insight. Its discovery was the great triumph of our Founding Fathers, voiced by William Penn when he said: "If we will not be governed by God, we must be governed by tyrants." Explaining the inalienable rights of men, Jefferson said, "The God who gave us life, gave us liberty at the same time." And it was George Washington who said that "of all the dispositions and habits which lead to political prosperity, religion and morality are indispensable supports."

And finally, that shrewdest of all observers of American democracy, Alexis de Tocqueville, put it eloquently after he had gone on a search for the secret of America's greatness and genius—and he said: "Not until I went into the churches of America and heard her pulpits aflame with righteousness did I understand the greatness and the genius of America ... America is good. And if America ever ceases to be good, America will cease to be great."

Well, I'm pleased to be here today with you who are keeping America great by keeping her good. Only through your work and prayers and those of millions of others can we hope to survive this perilous century and keep alive this experiment in liberty, this last best hope of man.

I want you to know that this administration is motivated by a political philosophy that sees the greatness of America in you, her people, and in your families, churches, neighborhoods, communities—the institutions that foster and nourish values like concern for others and respect for the rule of law under God.

Now, I don't have to tell you that this puts us in opposition to, or at least out of step with, a prevailing attitude of many who have turned to a modern-day secularism, discarding the tried and time-tested values upon which our very civilization is based. No matter how well intentioned, their value system is radically different from that of most Americans. And while they proclaim that they're freeing us from superstitions of the past, they've taken upon themselves the job of superintending us by government rule and regulation. Sometimes their voices are louder than ours, but they are not yet a majority.

An example of that vocal superiority is evident in a controversy now going on in Washington. And since I'm involved, I've been waiting to hear from the parents of young America. How far are they willing to go in giving to government their prerogatives as parents?

Let me state the case as briefly and simply as I can. An organization of citizens, sincerely motivated and deeply concerned about the increase in illegitimate births and abortions involving girls well below the age of consent, sometime ago established a nationwide network of clinics to offer help to these girls and, hopefully, alleviate this situation. Now, again, let me say, I do not fault their intent. However, in their well-intentioned effort, these clinics have decided to provide advice and birth control drugs and devices to underage girls without the knowledge of their parents.

For some years now, the Federal Government has helped with funds to subsidize these clinics. In providing for this, the Congress decreed that every effort would be made to maximize parental participation. Nevertheless, the drugs and devices are prescribed without getting parental consent or giving notification after they've done so. Girls termed "sexually active"—and that has replaced the word "promiscuous"—are given this help in order to prevent illegitimate birth or abortion.

Well, we have ordered clinics receiving Federal funds to notify the parents such help has been given. One of the Nation's leading newspapers has created the term "squeal rule" in editorializing against us for doing this, and we're being criticized for violating the privacy of young people. A judge has recently granted an injunction against an enforcement of our rule. I've watched TV panel shows discuss this issue, seen columnists pontificating on our error, but no one seems to mention morality as playing a part in the subject of sex.

Is all of Judeo-Christian tradition wrong? Are we to believe that something so sacred can be looked upon as a purely physical thing with no potential for emotional and psychological harm? And isn't it the parents' right to give counsel and advice to keep their children from making mistakes that may affect their entire lives?

Many of us in government would like to know what parents think about this intrusion in their family by government. We're going to fight in the courts. The right of parents and the rights of family take precedence over those of Washington-based bureaucrats and social engineers.

But the fight against parental notification is really only one example of many attempts to water down traditional values and even abrogate the original terms of American democracy. Freedom prospers when religion is vibrant and the rule of law under God is acknowledged. When our Founding Fathers passed the first amendment, they sought to protect churches from government interference. They never intended to construct a wall of hostility between government and the concept of religious belief itself.

The evidence of this permeates our history and our government. The Declaration of Independence mentions the Supreme Being no less than four times. "In God We Trust" is engraved on our coinage. The Supreme Court opens its proceedings with a religious invocation. And the Members of Congress open their sessions with a prayer. I just happen to believe the schoolchildren of the United States are entitled to the same privileges as Supreme Court Justices and Congressmen.

Last year, I sent the Congress a constitutional amendment to restore prayer to public schools. Already this session, there's growing bipartisan support for the amendment, and I am calling on the Congress to act speedily to pass it and to let our children pray.

Perhaps some of you read recently about the Lubbock school case, where a judge actually ruled that it was unconstitutional for a school district to give equal treatment to religious and nonreligious student groups, even when the group meetings were being held during the students' own time. The first amendment never intended to require government to discriminate against religious speech.

Senators Denton and Hatfield have proposed legislation in the Congress on the whole question of prohibiting discrimination against religious forms of student speech. Such legislation could go far to restore freedom of religious speech for public school students. And I hope the Congress considers these bills quickly. And with your help, I think it's possible we could also get the constitutional amendment through the Congress this year.

More than a decade ago, a Supreme Court decision literally wiped off the books of fifty States statutes protecting the rights of unborn children. Abortion on demand now takes the lives of up to one and a half million unborn children a year. Human life legislation ending this tragedy will some day pass the Congress, and you and I must never rest until it does. Unless and until it can be proven that the unborn child is not a living entity, then its right to life, liberty, and the pursuit of happiness must be protected.

You may remember that when abortion on demand began, many, and, indeed, I'm sure many of you, warned that the practice would lead to a decline in respect for human life, that the philosophical premises used to justify abortion on demand would ultimately be used to justify other attacks on the sacredness of human life—infanticide or mercy killing. Tragically enough, those warnings proved all too true. Only last year a court permitted the death by starvation of a handicapped infant.

I have directed the Health and Human Services Department to make clear to every health care facility in the United States that the Rehabilitation Act of 1973 protects all handicapped persons against discrimination based on handicaps, including infants. And we have taken the further step of requiring that each and every recipient of Federal funds who provides health care services to infants must post and keep posted in a conspicuous place a notice stating that "discriminatory failure to feed and care for handicapped infants in this facility is prohibited by Federal law." It also lists a 24-hour, toll-free number so that nurses and others may report violations in time to save the infant's life.

In addition, recent legislation introduced in the Congress by Representative Henry Hyde of Illinois not only increases restrictions on publicly financed abortions, it also addresses this whole problem of infanticide. I urge the Congress to begin hearings and to adopt legislation that will protect the right of life to all children, including the disabled or handicapped.

Now, I'm sure that you must get discouraged at times, but you've done better than you know, perhaps. There's a great spiritual awakening in America, a renewal of the traditional values that have been the bedrock of America's goodness and greatness.

One recent survey by a Washington-based research council concluded that Americans were far more religious than the people of other nations; 95 percent of those surveyed expressed a belief in God and a huge majority believed the Ten Commandments had real meaning in their lives. And another study has found that an overwhelming majority of Americans disapprove of adultery, teenage sex, pornography, abortion, and hard drugs. And this same study showed a deep reverence for the importance of family ties and religious belief.

I think the items that we've discussed here today must be a key part of the Nation's political agenda. For the first time the Congress is openly and seriously debating and dealing with the prayer and abortion issues—and that's enormous progress right there. I repeat: America is in the midst of a spiritual awakening and a moral renewal. And with your Biblical keynote, I say today, "Yes, let justice roll on like a river, righteousness like a never-failing stream."

Now, obviously, much of this new political and social consensus I've talked about is based on a positive view of American history, one that takes pride in our country's accomplishments and record. But we must never forget that no government schemes are going to perfect man. We know that living in this world means dealing with what philosophers would call the phenomenology of evil or, as theologians would put it, the doctrine of sin.

There is sin and evil in the world, and we're enjoined by Scripture and the Lord Jesus to oppose it with all our might. Our nation, too, has a legacy of evil with which it must deal. The glory of this land has been its capacity for transcending the moral evils of our past. For example, the long struggle of minority citizens for equal rights, once a source of disunity and civil war, is now a point of pride for all Americans. We must never go back. There is no room for racism, anti-Semitism, or other forms of ethnic and racial hatred in this country.

I know that you've been horrified, as have I, by the resurgence of some hate groups preaching bigotry and prejudice. Use the mighty voice of your pulpits and the powerful standing of your churches to denounce and isolate these hate groups in our midst. The commandment given us is clear and simple: "Thou shalt love thy neighbor as thyself."

But whatever sad episodes exist in our past, any objective observer must hold a positive view of American history, a history that has been the story of hopes fulfilled and dreams made into reality. Especially in this century, America has kept alight the torch of freedom—not just for ourselves but for millions of others around the world.

And this brings me to my final point today. During my first press conference as president, in answer to a direct question, I pointed out that, as good Marxist-Leninists, the Soviet leaders have openly and publicly declared that the only morality they recognize is that which will further their cause, which is world revolution. I think I should point out I was only quoting Lenin, their guiding spirit, who said in 1920 that they repudiate all morality that proceeds from supernatural ideas—that's their name for religion—or ideas that are outside class conceptions. Morality is entirely subordinate to the interests of class war. And everything is moral that is necessary for the annihilation of the old, exploiting social order and for uniting the proletariat.

Well, I think the refusal of many influential people to accept this elementary fact of Soviet doctrine illustrates an historical reluctance to see totalitarian powers for what they are. We saw this phenomenon in the 1930s. We see it too often today.

This doesn't mean we should isolate ourselves and refuse to seek an understanding with them. I intend to do everything I can to persuade them of our peaceful intent, to remind them that it was the West that refused to use its nuclear monopoly in the forties and fifties for territorial gain and which now proposes a 50 percent cut in strategic ballistic missiles and the elimination of an entire class of land-based, intermediate-range nuclear missiles.

At the same time, however, they must be made to understand we will never compromise our principles and standards. We will never give away our freedom. We will never abandon our belief in God. And we will never stop searching for a genuine peace. But we can assure none of these things America stands for through the so-called nuclear freeze solutions proposed by some.

The truth is that a freeze now would be a very dangerous fraud, for that is merely the illusion of peace. The reality is that we must find peace through strength. I would agree to a freeze if only we could freeze the Soviets' global desires. A freeze at current levels of weapons would remove any incentive for the Soviets to negotiate seriously in Geneva and virtually end our chances to achieve the major arms reductions which we have proposed. Instead, they would achieve their objectives through the freeze.

A freeze would reward the Soviet Union for its enormous and unparalleled military buildup. It would prevent the essential and long overdue modernization of United States and allied defenses and would leave our aging forces increasingly vulnerable. And an honest freeze would require extensive prior negotiations on the systems and numbers to be limited and on the measures to ensure effective verification and compliance. And the kind of a freeze that has been suggested would be virtually impossible to verify. Such a major effort would divert us completely from our current negotiations on achieving substantial reductions.

A number of years ago, I heard a young father, a very prominent young man in the entertainment world, addressing a tremendous gathering in California. It was during the time of the cold war, and communism and our own way of life were very much on people's minds. And he was speaking to that subject. And suddenly, though, I heard him saying, "I love my little girls more than anything—" And I said to myself, "Oh, no, don't. You can't—don't say that." But I had underestimated him. He went on: "I would rather see my little girls die now, still believing in God, than have them grow up under communism and one day die no longer believing in God."

There were thousands of young people in that audience. They came to their feet with shouts of joy. They had instantly recognized the profound truth in what he had said, with regard to the physical and the soul and what was truly important.

Yes, let us pray for the salvation of all of those who live in that totalitarian darkness—pray they will discover the joy of knowing God. But until they do, let us be aware that while they preach the supremacy of the state, declare its omnipotence over individual man, and predict its eventual domination of all peoples on the Earth, they are the focus of evil in the modern world.

It was C. S. Lewis who, in his unforgettable *Screwtape Letters*, wrote: "The greatest evil is not done now in those sordid 'dens of crime' that Dickens loved to paint. It is not even done in concentration camps and labor camps. In those we see its final result. But it is conceived and ordered (moved, seconded, carried and minuted) in clear, carpeted, warmed, and well-lighted offices, by quiet men with white collars and cut fingernails and smooth-shaven cheeks who do not need to raise their voice."

Well, because these "quiet men" do not "raise their voices," because they sometimes speak in soothing tones of brotherhood and peace, because, like other dictators before them, they're always making "their final territorial demand," some would have us accept them at their word and accommodate ourselves to their aggressive impulses. But if history teaches anything, it teaches that simple-minded appeasement or wishful thinking about our adversaries is folly. It means the betrayal of our past, the squandering of our freedom.

So, I urge you to speak out against those who would place the United States in a position of military and moral inferiority. You know, I've always believed that old Screwtape reserved his best efforts for those of you in the church. So, in your discussions of the nuclear freeze proposals, I urge you to beware the temptation of pride—the temptation of blithely declaring yourselves above it all and label both sides equally at fault, to ignore the facts of history and the aggressive impulses of an evil empire, to simply call the arms race a giant misunderstanding and thereby remove yourself from the struggle between right and wrong and good and evil.

I ask you to resist the attempts of those who would have you withhold your support for our efforts, this administration's efforts, to keep America strong and free, while we negotiate real and verifiable reductions in the world's nuclear arsenals and one day, with God's help, their total elimination.

While America's military strength is important, let me add here that I've always maintained that the struggle now going on for the world will never be decided by bombs or rockets, by armies or military might. The real crisis we face today is a spiritual one; at root, it is a test of moral will and faith.

Whittaker Chambers, the man whose own religious conversion made him a witness to one of the terrible traumas of our time, the Hiss-Chambers case, wrote that the crisis of the Western World exists to the degree in which the West is indifferent to God, the degree to which it collaborates in communism's attempt to make man stand alone without God. And then he said, for Marxism-Leninism is actually the second oldest faith, first proclaimed in the Garden of Eden with the words of temptation, "Ye shall be as gods."

The Western World can answer this challenge, he wrote, "but only provided that its faith in God and the freedom He enjoins is as great as communism's faith in Man."

I believe we shall rise to the challenge. I believe that communism is another sad, bizarre chapter in human history whose last pages even now are being written. I believe this because the source of our strength in the quest for human freedom is not material, but spiritual. And because it knows no limitation, it must terrify and ultimately triumph over those who would enslave their fellow man. For in the words of Isaiah: "He giveth power to the faint; and to them that have no might He increased strength ... But they that wait upon the Lord shall renew their strength; they shall mount up with wings as eagles; they shall run, and not be weary ... "

Yes, change your world. One of our Founding Fathers, Thomas Paine, said, "We have it within our power to begin the world over again." We can do it, doing together what no one church could do by itself.

God bless you, and thank you very much.

Original Draft of the "Evil Empire" Speech

Hearing the words of the Evil Empire speech was striking enough; seeing them in their original form is an altogether different experience.

The speech was written by one of Reagan's youngest and most talented speechwriters, Tony Dolan. As Dolan has always been quick to note, however, the speech is "totally Reagan"—it is "completely Reagan's."[187] That was true in part because Dolan notes that he could have never written the speech for anyone but Ronald Reagan; another president would not have accepted it, believed it, or had the courage to deliver it, particularly over the universal objections of his advisers. Dolan wrote it for Reagan based on Reagan.

But even then, as Dolan is quick to acknowledge, he was at best a coauthor. This was not merely because Dolan had written words that embodied the essence of Reagan, or had borrowed words Reagan himself had written in earlier self-written orations—"They're the president's phrases," Dolan told me—but because Reagan had written at least half the speech himself.

This is evident in the March 5 draft of the speech, which today is on file with Reagan's handwriting at the Reagan Library. Ronald Reagan made so many changes, edits, removals, and additions that it is fair to call him the coauthor.[188] There are numerous classic Reagan anecdotes penciled in by Reagan himself throughout the text.

An examination of Reagan's handwritten edits of the speech shows that the president himself slashed over a dozen entire paragraphs from Dolan's original draft. He eliminated numerous sentences and hundreds of words. It is difficult to quantify handwritten lines, but it looks like Reagan himself penciled in over a dozen full, new paragraphs as well as at least an extra thirty complete lines of text. Reagan added and removed entire pages of text. Moreover, the Reagan changes often came in the most significant spots, making the speech so memorable.

Take a look for yourself. What follows is the original draft of the speech, along with President Reagan's many changes. The draft today quietly resides in Box 9, Folder 150 of the Presidential Handwriting File at the Ronald Reagan Library.

If this comes out short — too short maybe we can paste back the "crime section" (Dolan/AB)
March 5, 1983
Noon

RR

PRESIDENTIAL ADDRESS: NATIONAL ASSOCIATION OF EVANGELICALS
ORLANDO, FLORIDA
TUESDAY, MARCH 8, 1983

~~Nancy and~~ I ^AM^ ~~are~~ delighted to be here today. Those of you in the National Association of Evangelicals are known for your spiritual and humanitarian work -- and I would be especially remiss if I did not discharge right now one personal debt of gratitude.

Thank you for your prayers. Nancy and I have felt their presence many times in many ways. Believe me, for us they have made all the difference. The other day in the East Room *of the White House* someone asked me whether I was aware of all the people out there praying for the President. *YES I AM — BECAUSE I'VE FELT IT + I believe in intercessionary pray* I was touched, of course, ~~but I'll tell you~~ *But I couldn't help but say to that questioner that if sometime what I told him: Thank you but please keep it up. And when* ~~when he was praying the great~~ *you're at it, if you got* a busy signal ~~sometimes, keep trying.~~ *I guess it was me*

"It ~~just means I'm~~ in there ahead of ~~you~~ *him*. *I feel as Abe Lincoln felt when I said, I have been driven many times to my knees by the overwhelming conviction that I had no where to go."* From the joy and good feeling of this conference ~~we leave I go~~ *To I don't know why that* ~~for the hurly-burly of~~ a political reception ~~for the Florida GOP.~~ *scheduling reminds me of a story but it does.* ~~You can see it's a day of contrasts; (it reminds me of a story I may just tell the folks over at that reception. It seems this~~

An evangelical minister and ^a^ politician ~~both died and went to~~ Heavens gate *arrived at* ~~together,~~ St. Peter took them in hand to show them their new quarters. He took the minister to a small room with just a bed *a single chair,* and table. ~~So naturally when~~ *The* politician *was a little* ~~saw the modest quarters of this holy man he was pretty~~ worried about what was in store for him. *And he couldn't believe it when* ~~Much to his surprise,~~ St. Peter *stopped before* ~~took him to~~ a great mansion, with beautiful grounds and many servants and told him all this

Page 2

would be his. ~~So naturally, the politician said:~~ *The politician said* "But how can you give me this mansion ~~and only a small place to that good~~ *while that good & holy man only gets a single room.*

~~minister?"~~

St. Peter ~~replied,~~ *said,* "Oh, ~~don't worry, he's an evangelical, here, we've got thousands & thousands of clergy — we've got plenty of them up here. But~~ you're the first politician ~~we've ever had.~~ *who ever made it.*

Now I don't want to contribute to a stereotype. I tell you truly there are

~~I like that story. Those of us in the political world need~~ *a great many God fearing, dedicated, noble men & women in public life. Yes we need* ~~to be reminded that our fast-paced existence can sometimes be an~~

~~obstacle to quiet reflection and deep commitment, that we can~~ *YOUR HELP TO KEEP US EVER MINDFUL OF* ~~easily forget~~ the ideas and principles that brought us into the public arena in the first place. The basis of those ideals and principles is a commitment to freedom and personal liberty, a commitment that itself is grounded in the much deeper realization: that freedom prospers only where the blessings of God are avidly sought and humbly acknowledged.

The American experiment in democracy rests on this insight; its discovery was the great triumph of our Founding Fathers *voiced long* *Wm. Penn:* "Men who will not be ruled by God will be ruled by tyrants," ~~William Penn said.~~ Explaining the inalienable rights of men, Jefferson ~~remarked,~~ *said* "The God who gave us life, gave us liberty at the same time." And it was George Washington who said that "of all the disposition and habits which lead to political prosperity, religion and morality are indispensable supports."

And finally, that shrewdest of all observers of American democracy, Alexis de Tocqueville, put it eloquently *after he had gone on a search for the secret of American greatness & genius.*

~~I sought for the greatness and genius of America in fertile fields and boundless forests, it was not there. I sought for it in her free schools and her institutions of learning; it was not there.~~ I sought

Page 3

~~for it in her matchless Constitution and democratic~~
~~congress; it was not there.~~ Not until I went to the
churches of America and ~~found them aflame with~~ HEARD HER PULPITS AFLAME
WITH righteousness did I understand the greatness and genius
of America. America is great because America is good.
AND IF → ~~When~~ America ever ceases to be good, America will cease to
be great.")

~~That is why~~ I am ~~so~~ pleased to be here today with ~~the people~~ YES
who are ~~in the business of~~ keeping America great by keeping her
good. Only through your work and prayers and those of millions
of others can we hope to survive this perilous century and keep
alive this experiment in liberty, this last best hope of man-
~~called America~~.

I want you to know this Administration is motivated by a
political philosophy that sees the greatness of America in you,
her people, and in your families, churches, neighborhoods,
communities -- the institutions that foster and nourish values
like concern for others and respect for the rule of law under
God.

Now I don't have to tell you that ~~our pursuit of~~ this
OR AT LEAST OUT OF STEP WITH A
~~philosophy~~ puts us in opposition to ~~the~~ prevailing attitude of
who have turned to a modern day secularism, discarding
many ~~of those in government, educational foundations and~~
the tried & time tested values upon which our very civilization is based.
~~institutions; and significant sectors of the media. The views of~~
No matter how
~~such groups, however~~ well intentioned, ~~are deeply secularist and~~
And while they proclaim they are freeing us
~~decidedly liberal;~~ their value system is radically different from
that of most Americans. ~~Because they view everyday Americans as~~
from superstitions of the past
~~wanton and unwise,~~ they have taken upon themselves the job of
and by govt. rule & regulation
~~regulating, overseeing and~~ superintending ~~the people from~~
~~Washington~~.

Page 4

Some times their voices are louder than ours but they are not yet a majority.

An example of that vocal superiority is evident in a controversy now going on in Wash. Since I'm involved I've been waiting to hear from the parents of young America - How far are they willing to go in giving ~~up~~ their prerogatives as parents?

Let me state the case as briefly & simply as I can. An organization of citizens sincerely motivated & deeply concerned about the increase in illegitimate births and abortions involving girls well below the age of consent established clinics that often help to these girls and hopefully to alleviate this situation.

Again let me say I do not fault their intent. However in their well intentioned effort these clinics provide advice and birth control drugs & devices to under age girls without the knowledge of their parents. For some years now the Federal govt. has helped with funds to subsidize these clinics. In providing for this the Congress decreed that "every effort would be made to maximize parental participation." Never the less the drugs & devices are prescribed without getting parental consent or giving notification. Girls so termed "sexually active" — that has replaced the word "promiscuous" — are given this help in order to prevent illegitimate birth or abortion.

We have ordered clinics receiving Fed. funds to notify the parents such help has been given. One of the nations leading newspapers has created the term "squeal rule" in editorializing against us and we are being criticized for violating the privacy of young people. A judge has granted an injunction against enforcement of our rule.

I have watched TV panel shows discuss this issue, have read columns pontificating on our error but no one seems to mention morality as playing a part in the subject of sex.

P.S.

Is all of Judeo-Christian tradition wrong? Are we to believe that something so sacred can be looked upon as a purely physical thing with no potential for emotional & psychological harm? And isn't it the parents right to give counsel & advice to keep their children from making mistakes that may affect their entire lives?

~~We are going to fight the court decision but~~ Many of us in govt. would like to know ~~what~~ parents think about this intrusion in their family by govt. ~~While we're at it we might also ask why it is~~ that an underage girl can take advantage of our welfare regulations to obtain an abortion without her parents knowledge or consent. ~~Yet the consent~~ ~~have the forcible someone with out parental consent~~ Yet parental permission is required for any other ~~kind of operation~~.

Yes we all know there are parents who for whatever reason have not communicated with their children as they should but there are millions & millions who have.

Page 6

Well, I say We fight our battle in the courts. I say the rule always. And I say The rights of parents and the rights of family take precedence over those of Washington-based bureaucrats and social engineers.

But parental notification is really only one example of many attempts to water down traditional values and even abrogate the original terms of American democracy. As I mentioned before, nothing could be more deeply engrained into the American political consensus than the realization that Freedom prospers when religion is vibrant and the rule of law under God acknowledged. When our Founding Fathers passed the first amendment they sought to protect churches from Government interference. They never meant to construct a wall of hostility between Government and the concept of religious belief itself.

The evidence of this permeates our history and our government: The Declaration of Independence mentions the Supreme Being no less than four times; "In God We Trust" is engraved on our coinage; the Supreme Court opens its proceedings with a "religious" invocation; and the Members of Congress open their sessions with a prayer. I just happen to believe the school children of the United States are entitled to the same privileges as Supreme Court Justices and Congressmen. Last year, I sent the Congress a constitutional amendment to restore prayer to public schools. This week I am resubmitting that amendment and calling on the Congress to act speedily to pass it. Let our children pray.

Page 7

(But in the controversy over the prayer amendment, we see once again that will to power that has characterized so much of the ~~liberal social philosophy that~~ dominated American *new secularism.* ~~intellectual life in the fifties and sixties.~~ Many Advocates of ~~liberal and~~ so-called progressive education hoped that the schools would become laboratories where school children could be removed from traditional influences and taught instead the wonders of value-free science and moral relativism.

~~Now we know that what happened to American education as it increasingly fell under the influence of this "social science mentality.~~ [w]As influence of parents and teachers declined, so did excellence and discipline -- and ~~Americas school~~ children *one formed one* ~~learned~~ *learning* less ~~and less.~~

As you all know, there has been a rebellion among parents and teachers against these lax educational standards and once again basic learning is being increasingly stressed in our schools.

Similarly, the attempt to prohibit the acknowledgement of God in the classroom has come under heavy fire. By overwhelming margins, the American people want prayer returned to the classroom and have been voting for candidates who support that amendment.

Unfortunately, however, this hasn't discouraged the small group of elitists on the left who still want to impose their ~~value system on the vast majority of Americans.~~) Perhaps some of you read recently about the Lubbock school case where a judge actually ruled that it was unconstitutional for a school district

Page 8

to give equal treatment to religious and nonreligious student
groups, even when the group meetings were ~~held~~ during the students'
own time. ~~You can see, can't you, how the first amendment has
been stood on its head, how~~ A constitutional provision designed
to promote religious expression has been used to stifle that
expression? ~~And you can see, can't you, the irony of those who
call themselves "liberals" using their position of power~~ to deny
to millions the time-honored right of religious expression in
public places?

~~I think you should know that both~~ Senators Denton and
Hatfield have proposed legislation in the Congress on the whole
question of prohibiting discrimination against religious forms of
student speech. I strongly support that legislation, and, with
your help, I think it's possible we could also get the
constitutional amendment through the Congress this year.

~~And let me add here that, like you, I have been deeply
concerned about recent controversies in several States between
religious schools and State educational authorities. No one
questions the right of the individual States to have a voice in
establishing certain minimum standards for the education of our
children. But, on the other hand, religious schools are entitled
to make basic decisions about their curriculum and not be forced
to march in lockstep to the directives of State bureaucrats.

Now in discussing these instances of the arbitrary
imposition of liberal views, we would be remiss not to mention a
Supreme Court decision more than a decade ago that, quite
literally, wiped off the books the statutes of 50 States~~

Page 9 *More than a decade ago a Supreme Ct. decision literally wiped off the books of 50 states, statutes*

protecting the rights of unborn children. "Abortion on demand"

~~is a great moral evil that~~ *morin* takes the lives of 1½ million unborn

children a year. Human life legislation ending this tragedy will

someday pass the Congress -- and you and I must never rest until

it does. *Unless & until* ~~Until unless it can be proven that the unborn child is not a living~~ *entity, then it's right to life, liberty & the pursuit of happiness must be protected*

You may remember that when abortion on demand began many, *indeed,*

I'm sure many of you ~~religious leaders~~ warned that the practice would lead to a

decline in respect for human life, that the philosophical

premises used to justify abortion on demand would ultimately be

used to justify other attacks on the sacredness of human life,

~~even~~ infanticide or mercy killing. ~~When these warnings were~~

~~first spoken, many of those in the intelligensia and the glitter~~ *THOSE WARNINGS*

~~set scoffed at them. But,~~ Tragically enough, ~~they~~ proved all too

true: only last year a court ~~in Indiana issued an~~ order

permitting ~~permitting~~ the death by starvation of a handicapped infant.

~~When that baby's death came to light,~~ *HAVE* I directed the Health

and Human Services Department to make clear to every health care

facility in the United States that the Rehabilitation Act of 1973

protects <u>all</u> handicapped persons against discrimination based on

handicaps, <u>including</u> infants. And we have taken the further step

of requiring that each and every recipient of Federal funds who

provides health care services must post and keep posted in a

conspicuous place a notice stating that "discriminatory failure

to feed and care for handicapped infants in this facility is

prohibited by Federal law."

In addition, recent legislation introduced in the Congress

by Representative Henry Hyde not only increases restrictions on

Page 10

publicly-financed abortions, it also addresses this whole problem

of infanticide. I urge the Congress to begin hearings ~~soon on~~ and

~~this legislation, to address the problems of infanticide, to~~

adopt legislation that will protect the right of all children, ^LIFE TO

including the disabled or handicapped, ~~to the right to life.~~

~~Now in surveying the effect of several decades of liberal,~~

~~secularist philosophy -- the wreckage, for example, left by the~~

~~decisions like those on abortion and school prayer -- it is easy~~

~~to grow discouraged. But we must never forget that we now stand~~

~~at a turning point, a time when the old liberalism -- decadent~~

~~and dying -- is being replaced by a new political consensus, a~~

~~consensus that wants Government to perform its legitimate duties,~~

~~such as maintaining domestic peace and our national security, but~~

~~otherwise to leave the people alone.~~

I'm sure you must get discouraged at times but

~~Along with this return to limited Government,~~ there is a

great spiritual awakening in America, ~~and~~ a renewal of the

traditional values that have been the bedrock of America's

goodness and greatness.

(One recent survey ~~of thousands of Americans~~ by a Washington

based research council concluded that Americans were far more

religious than the people of other nations; 95 percent of those

surveyed expressed a belief in God and a huge majority believed

the Ten Commandments had real meaning for their lives.

Another study ~~of 3,000 Americans by Connecticut Mutual Life~~ has found that an overwhelming majority

~~Insurance found that -- in contrast to the views of the elites~~

~~mentioned earlier -- the following practices were found wrong~~

~~by large majorities of average Americans: adultery, 85 percent,~~

of Americans disapprove of adultery, ~~hard drugs,~~

teen age sex, pornography, abortion + hard drugs.

Page 11

~~hard drugs, 84 percent; homosexuality, #1 percent; sex before~~ 6,
~~#1 percent; abortion, 65 percent; and pornography, 69 percent.~~
And this same study showed a deep reverence for the importance of
family ties and religious belief.)

~~So~~ I think the items we have discussed ^are^ today are the
political agenda of the future. ~~Remember,~~ For the first time the
Congress is openly and seriously debating and dealing with the
prayer and abortion issues -- that's enormous progress right
there. I repeat: America is in the midst of a spiritual
awakening and a moral renewal. With your biblical keynote, I say
today let "justice roll on like a river, righteousness like a
never failing stream."

Now, obviously, much of this new political and social
consensus I have talked about is based on a positive view of
American history, one that takes pride in our country's
accomplishments and record. But we must never forget ~~an~~
~~important distinction between our moral philosophy and that of~~
~~the liberal secularists. Unlike them, we~~ know that no Government
schemes are going to perfect man; we know that living in this
world means dealing with what philosophers would call the
phenomenology of evil or, as ~~the~~ theologians would put it, the
doctrine of sin.

There is sin, ~~there is~~ ^and^ evil in ~~this~~ ^The^ world, and we are
enjoined by scripture and the Lord Jesus to oppose it with all
our might. ~~And that is why in talking about America we must~~
~~never forget that, like any other human entity,~~ Our Nation, too,
has a legacy of evil with which it must deal.

Page 12

~~Now~~, The glory of this land has been its capacity for transcending the moral evils of our past. For example, the long struggle of minority citizens for equal rights, once a source of disunity and civil war, is now a point of pride for all Americans. We must never go back. There is no room for racism, anti-semitism or other forms of ethnic and racial hatred in this country. I know you have been horrified, as have I, by the resurgence of some hate groups preaching bigotry and prejudice. ~~Today, I urge you:~~ Use the mighty voice of your pulpits and the powerful standing of your churches to denounce and isolate these hate groups in our midst. *The commandment given us is clear & simple —* ~~We are to love our neighbors as~~ *"Thou shalt love thy neighbor as thyself"*

~~[And I want to mention today another dark legacy of our past -- one that we are also now attempting to address in Washington. For many years in America we tolerated the existence of powerful syndicates of organized crime. As the years went by, these national syndicates increased in power, influence, and sophistication. Recently, in the enormous growth of the illegal drug trade, we have seen the tragic results of this permissiveness and the climate of professional lawlessness it fostered. Only a short time ago, this trade was spreading murder and mayhem throughout South Florida. Today, through the South Florida Task Force headed by Vice President Bush, we have a handle on it. We've cracked down on this drug trade in Florida, and now we're bringing on 200 new prosecutors and 1,260 new investigators to extend that task force model to 12 other regions throughout the United States.]~~

Page 13

Yes, we are going after the drug cartels. But we're not going to stop there. Through a new presidential commission and several other initiatives, we intend to expose and prosecute the infrastructure of organized crime itself. We mean to cripple their enterprises, dry up their profits, and put their leaders behind bars where they belong.

But whatever sad episodes exist in our past, any objective observer must hold a positive view of American history, a history that has been the story of hopes fulfilled and dreams made into reality. Especially in this century, America has kept alight the torch of freedom -- not just for ourselves but for millions of others around the world. And this brings me to my final point today, and, by the way, it's another illustration of the gulf between the views of the professional elitists and those of everyday Americans.

During my first press conference as President _in answer to a direct question_ I pointed out that as good Marxists-Leninists the Soviet leaders have "openly and publicly declared that the only morality they recognize is that _which is moral revolution._ what will further their cause, meaning they reserve unto _And I quoted statements by previous leaders in which they were specific as to_ themselves the right to commit any crime, to lie, to _the things we would consider criminal or immoral but which would be justified if_ cheat — and that is moral, not immoral." I said that we _done to further socialism._ would do well to keep this in mind during our negotiations with them. _Somehow this was translated to be accusations by some rather_ the Soviets. _than a quote of their own words._

Well, once again this caused a stir. I saw several accounts that truncated my remarks and suggested they were nothing more than name-calling. Other accounts suggested that it was a breach of diplomacy to be that candid about the Soviets.

This misrepresentation is frequently repeated accompanied by a charge that my harsh & intemperate accusations are making it impossible for us to have any kind of understanding with the Soviet leadership.

Page 14

Now -- putting aside for the moment the fact that ~~the~~ some

pundits and opinion makers are rarely upset when the Soviets say

much worse about us everyday in their press -- I think I should

point out I was only quoting Lenin, ~~a saint,~~ THEIR a guiding spirit ~~to~~

~~the Soviet leadership~~, who wrote in 1920: "We repudiate all
(their term for our religion)
morality that proceeds from supernatural ideas or ideas that are

outside class conceptions. (Morality is entirely subordinate to

the interests of class war. Everything is moral that is

necessary for the annihilation of the old exploiting social order

and for uniting the proletariat.")

I think the refusal of many influential people to accept
FACT OF   DOCTRINE
this elementary ~~insight into~~ Soviet ~~behavior~~ illustrates an

historical reluctance to see totalitarian powers for what they

are. We saw this phenomenon in the 1930's; we see it too often

today, as in many aspects of the nuclear freeze movement. *This does not
mean we should isolate ourselves and refuse to seek an understanding with them.*
~~But surely, just as we look back in wonder at the~~
I intend to do everything I can to persuade them of our peaceful intent; to remind them
~~self-deception of the 1930's, future historians, looking back at~~

~~our time, will be shocked by the naiveté and moral blindness of~~

~~the unilateral disarmers. (Surely they will note the real~~

~~proportions of the threat to peace,~~ that it _was_ the West that

refused to use its nuclear monopoly in the forties and fifties

for territorial gain and which now proposes 50-percent cuts in

strategic ballistic missiles and the elimination of an entire

class of land-based, intermediate-range nuclear missiles. -- ~~and~~

that it was _not_ the West that intervened by military proxy in

Angola, in Ethiopia, in South Yemen or Central America; that it

was _not_ the West that invaded Afghanistan, suppressed Polish

*At the same time however they must be made to understand
we will never compromise our principles & standards. We will never
give away our freedom. We will never _____ our belief in God.*

14 A

A number of years ago ~~at the height of the cold war a young man who had achieved stardom in the entertainment world, appeared at a giant rally in Los Angeles. There were~~

A number of years ago I heard a young father addressing a tremendous gathering in Calif. It was during the time of the cold war when communism and our own way of life were very much on peoples minds. He was speaking to that subject. Suddenly I heard him saying: "I love my little girls more than anything in the world, but I would rather see them ~~dead~~ — I thought oh no dont say that. But I had under estimated him. He went on: "I would rather see them die now still believing in God, ~~as they are~~, than have them grow up under communism and one day die no longer believing in God."

There were thousands of young people in that audience. They came to their feet with shouts of joy. They recognized the profound truth in what he had said.

Let us pray for the salvation of all those who live in that totalitarian darkness — pray they will discover the joy of knowing God.

But until they do let us be aware that while they —

Page 15

Solidarity, used forced labor, or waged chemical and toxic
warfare in Afghanistan and Southeast Asia.)

Surely, these historians will find in the councils of the
Marxist-Leninists -- who preached the supremacy of the state, who
declared its omnipotence over individual man, who predicted its
eventual domination of all peoples of the Earth -- surely
historians will see there they are . . . the focus of evil in the modern
world. It was C. S. Lewis who in his unforgettable <u>Screwtape</u>
<u>Letters</u> wrote:

> "The greatest evil is not now done in those sordid
> 'dens of crime' that Dickens loved to paint. It is not
> done even in concentration camps and labor camps -- in
> those we see its final result. But it is conceived and
> ordered (moved, seconded, carried and minuted) in
> clear, carpeted, warmed and well-lighted offices by
> quiet men with white collars and cut fingernails and
> smooth-shaven cheeks who do not need to raise their
> voices."

Because these "quiet men" do not "raise their voices," because
they sometimes speak in soothing tones of brotherhood and peace,
because, like other dictators before them, they are always making
"their final territorial demand," some would have us accept them
at their word and accommodate ourselves to their aggressive
impulses. But, if history teaches anything, it teaches:
simple-minded appeasement or self-delusion about our adversaries
is folly -- it means the betrayal of our past, the squandering of
our freedom.

So I urge you to speak out against those who would place the
United States in a position of military inferiority to the Soviet
Union. You know, I have always believed that old Screwtape
reserves his best efforts for those of you in the Church. So in

Page 16

your discussions of the nuclear freeze proposals, I urge you to
beware the temptation of pride -- the temptation to blithely
declare yourselves above it all and label both sides equally at
fault, to ignore the facts of history and the aggressive impulses
of an evil empire, to simply call the arms race a giant
misunderstanding and thereby remove yourself from the struggle
between right and wrong, good and evil.

I ask you to resist the attempts of those who would have you
bargain away, for the sake of a few glowing minutes on the
nightly news and a little cooing from the glitter set, your vital
withhold your support for this Administration's efforts to keep America strong
and free, and the while we negotiate real and verifiable reductions in the
world's nuclear arsenals and one day with seek help their total elimination.

While America's military strength is important, let me add
here that I have always maintained that the struggle now going on
for the world will never be decided by bombs or rockets, by
armies or military might. For The real crisis we face today is a
spiritual one; at root, it is a test of moral will and faith.

(Whittaker Chambers, the man whose own religious conversion
made him a "witness" to one of the terrible traumas of our age,
the Hiss Chambers case, wrote that the crisis of the Western
world exists to the degree in which the West is indifferent to
God, the degree to which it collaborates in Communism's attempt
to make man stand alone without God. For Marxism-Leninism is
actually the second oldest faith, he said, first proclaimed in
the Garden of Eden with the words of temptation: "Ye shall be as
gods."

Page 17

The Western world can answer this challenge, he wrote, "but only provided that its faith in God and the freedom he enjoins is as great as Communism's faith in man."

I believe we shall rise to this challenge; I believe that Communism is another sad, bizarre chapter in human history whose last pages even now are being written. I believe this because the source of our strength in the quest for human freedom is not material but spiritual, and, because it knows no limitation, it must terrify and ultimately triumph over those who would enslave their fellow man. For, in the words of Isaiah:

"He giveth power to the faint, and to them that have no might, He increased their strength . . . but they that wait upon the Lord shall renew their strength . . . they shall mount up with wings as eagles. They shall run and not be weary . . ."

Thank you and God bless you.

Acknowledgments

This book began as a paper and lecture for an April 2012 conference on conservatism sponsored by the Center for Vision & Values at Grove City College, a think tank of which I'm the executive director. My work at the center, and ability to still find time to write, would be impossible without the stellar support of my outstanding supporting cast: Lee Wishing, Brenda Vinton, and Cory Shreckengost—not to mention the tremendous leadership of Grove City College's dedicated president, alumnus, and biggest booster, Dick Jewell.

I began the process of turning the paper and lecture into a book with the encouragement of Kimberly Begg of the Young America's Foundation, which hosted me as the keynote speaker for the 2012 annual New Jersey Reagan Day Dinner. Kimberly thought it would make a good book, and I hope she turned out to be correct.

As I continued to deliver the lecture at various other venues and refine the concepts, others listened and provided suggestions for improvement. Frank Gaffney heard me list my *ten* Reagan principles at CPAC in 2012. He told me I had neglected "peace through strength." Leave it to Frank to notice that omission. Of course, he was exactly right, and I'm most grateful for his crucial recommendation.

The book finally came together at another magical CPAC moment, this one in March 2013. Eric Kampmann introduced himself to me during a book signing and told me of the new publishing venture by himself and the terrific Al Regnery. It sounded promising, and I recommended they consider a book manuscript by a friend of mine. A week or so later, it hit me that my own manuscript, then titled, *What Is a Reagan Conservative?* might be of interest to Eric and Al. I e-mailed them the manuscript. They immediately responded. The rest is history.

Is it not perfect that it took CPAC to bring it all together? Ronald Reagan would be pleased.

I'm thankful for the last-minute research assistance of Alex Welch and Caleb Parke, two super Grove City College students. Caleb's searches on Reagan and the family were a huge help. For earlier research on Reagan and the Founders, I'd like to acknowledge Jarrett Skorup, a talented former student fellow at the Center for Vision & Values, who today does excellent work for the Mackinac Center, and Mallory Sampson, another former student. They searched the *Public Papers of the Presidents* for quotations on the Founders when I first dug in to the subject a few years back. Finally, I'm indebted to Andrew Busch for his excellent work on budget and economic data cited in this book, which (in one particular section) I borrowed from extensively.

I also thank Megan Trank and Felicia Minerva at Beaufort Books for their terrific editorial, copy-editing, and promotional work. They do a good job.

It is my sincerest hope that conservatives nationwide, and would-be conservatives and even nonconservatives everywhere, find this book a valuable teaching tool not only on Ronald Reagan but America.

About the Author

D r. Paul Kengor is professor of political science at Grove City College in Grove City, Pennsylvania, and executive director of the college's Center for Vision & Values (www.visionandvalues. org and www.faithandfreedom.com). He is also a visiting fellow at the Hoover Institution. Kengor's articles have appeared everywhere, from the popular press to scholarly journals and across the ideological spectrum—*USA Today, New York Times, National Review, Wall Street Journal, American Spectator,* CNN.com, FoxNews. com, *The Guardian, Christianity Today, National Catholic Register, Jewish World Review, International Herald Tribune, Political Science Quarterly,* and *Presidential Studies Quarterly,* to name a few. He has been quoted in publications ranging from the *Washington Post* to *Pravda.* He provides frequent commentary on radio and television: MSNBC, Fox News, C-SPAN, *The O'Reilly Factor, Fox & Friends,* the BBC, NPR, Mark Levin, Sean Hannity, Glenn Beck, Bill Bennett, Michael Medved, and many more. He does a weekly commentary for EWTN radio and Ave Maria Radio Network.

Kengor's essays and various chapters have been published in academic presses such as Oxford University Press, Columbia University Press, and Harvard University Press. A *New York Times* best-selling author, Kengor's most recent books include *The Communist: Frank Marshall Davis; The Untold Story of Barack Obama's Mentor* and *Dupes: How America's Adversaries Have Manipulated Progressives for a Century,* both based on extensive Soviet archival and Communist Party USA research.

Professor Kengor is an internationally recognized authority on Ronald Reagan. His best sellers *God and Ronald Reagan* and *The Crusader: Ronald Reagan & the Fall of Communism* revealed the Reagan that so many never knew. They have been translated into multiple languages, particularly in former communist countries, and are the basis for a major upcoming Hollywood "bio-pic" titled *Reagan: The Movie*. Kengor is also the biographer of close Reagan friend, aide, and confidante Bill Clark. He published (with coauthor Patricia Clark Doerner) *The Judge: William P. Clark, Ronald Reagan's Top Hand*, a long-awaited biography of Reagan's most influential foreign-policy adviser, a man crucial to Reagan's effort to end Soviet communism. Kengor is currently completing an edited volume on the Reagan presidency for Harvard University Press.

Dr. Kengor spent many summers researching Ronald Reagan at the Reagan Library, in Reagan's hometown, and in Soviet and other archives. He has spoken on Reagan at the Reagan Library, the Reagan Ranch Center, the National Presbyterian Church, the National Press Club, the Heritage Foundation, CPAC, Young America's Foundation, Intercollegiate Studies Institute, Leadership Institute, American Enterprise Institute, University of Virginia, Eureka College, Franciscan University, the College of William & Mary, and numerous other venues.

Kengor is nationally known for his work on the American presidency. He served on the editorial board of *Presidential Studies Quarterly*, the flagship academic publication on the presidency. He is one of the select group of presidential scholars to participate in C-SPAN's highly regarded ranking of American presidents.

Kengor received his doctorate from the University of Pittsburgh's Graduate School of Public and International Affairs and his master's degree from American University's School of International Service. He holds an honorary doctorate from Franciscan University in Steubenville, Ohio. A native of western Pennsylvania, Kengor lives in Grove City, Pennsylvania, with his wife and their seven children.

Notes

1 "Zogby Interactive: Reagan, FDR Top Greatness Poll of Presidents Since World War II," *Zogby.com*, February 21, 2011.

2 Reagan rates among the top ten most successful presidents even in surveys of presidential scholars, who self-identify as "liberal" over "conservative" typically by margins of two to one. Starting in 1999, C-SPAN began surveying presidential scholars every ten years. The 2009 survey by C-SPAN, released for Presidents' Day 2009, which included sixty-five well-known presidential scholars, ranked Reagan tenth most successful, knocking Lyndon Johnson out of the top ten, and behind Woodrow Wilson at ninth.

3 The survey was conducted by Kelton Research for the National Geographic Channel. See Kenneth T. Walsh, "1980s Nostalgia: Poll Finds Reagan Beats Obama in a Landslide," *U.S. News & World Report*, April 10, 2013. Also see Paul Kengor, "The End of the Reagan Era?," exclusive to *American Spectator*, January 21, 2013.

4 On this, see George W. Bush's November 2003 speech to the National Endowment for Democracy and my article "The 'March of Freedom' from Reagan to Bush," *Policy Review*, December 2007 / January 2008.

5 Reagan, "Remarks at a Dinner Marking the Tenth Anniversary of the Heritage Foundation," Washington, DC, October 3, 1983.

6 Between 1974 and 1988, Reagan missed only the 1976 and 1980 meetings of CPAC, in both cases because he was in New Hampshire campaigning for the presidency. James C. Roberts, ed., *A City Upon a Hill: Speeches by Ronald Reagan Before the Conservative Political Action Conference* (Washington, DC: The American Studies Center, 1989).

7 Kirk's leading conservative works include *The Conservative Mind*, *The Roots of American Order*, and (among others) *The American Cause*. All are highly recommended for understanding true conservatism.

8 Reagan, "Remarks at the Annual Conservative Political Action Conference," Washington, DC, February 6, 1977.

9 On this see Lee Edwards, *William F. Buckley Jr.: The Making of a Movement* (Wilmington, DE: ISI Books, 2010).

10 Typically, the range is 35–40 percent of Americans who call themselves conservative versus 20–25 percent who call themselves liberal, even at times of seeming liberal ascendancy. A major Gallup poll conducted from January to May 2009, amid Barack Obama's first inauguration and at the height of "Obama mania," found more self-described conservatives than liberals not only by a margin of 40 percent to 21 percent but in literally all fifty states, from California to Massachusetts—the same electorate that chose Obama. For analysis, see Paul Kengor, "The End of the Reagan Era?," *American Spectator*, January 21, 2013; and Paul Kengor, "An Obama-Reagan Presidency?," February 13, 2009, posted at the website of the Center for Vision & Values.

11 Reagan, "Remarks at the Annual Conservative Political Action Conference," Washington, DC, February 20, 1987.

12 Reagan, "Remarks at the Annual Conservative Political Action Conference," Washington, DC, February 11, 1988.

13 Reagan, "Remarks at the Annual Conservative Political Action Conference," Washington, DC, February 6, 1977.

14 Likewise worth considering are the ten principles of conservative thought devised by the great conservative thinker Russell Kirk. These ten are listed at the website of the Russell Kirk Center: *www.kirkcenter.org/index.php/thought*.

15 Reagan was a great friend of Grove City College throughout its battle for freedom in higher education against the dictates of the federal government. That fight eventually took Grove City College all the way to the U.S. Supreme Court in 1984. All along, Reagan stood by the college. For more, see Lee Edwards, *Freedom's College: The History of Grove City College* (Washington, DC: Regnery, 2000).

16 Reagan, "Remarks at the Annual Meeting of the U.S. Chamber of Commerce," April 26, 1982.

17 Reagan, "Radio Address on Small Business," May 14, 1983.

18 Reagan, "Address to the Nation on the Eve of the Presidential Election," November 5, 1984.

19 Reagan, "Remarks at the Annual Convention of the Lions Club International," Dallas, TX, June 21, 1985.

20 Reagan, "State of the Union Address," January 25, 1983.

21 Reagan, "Address to the United Nations General Assembly," September 21, 1987.

22 Reagan, "Remarks at the Conservative Political Action Conference," Washington, DC, February 20, 1987.

23 Ibid.

24 Reagan, "Westminster Address in London," June 8, 1982.

25 Reagan, "Radio Address on Solidarity and U.S. Relations with Poland," October 9, 1982.

26 Reagan, "Remarks to Citizens in Hambach, Federal Republic of Germany," May 6, 1985.

27 Reagan, "Remarks to Soviet Dissidents at Spaso House in Moscow," May 30, 1988.

28 Reagan, "Address to a Special Session of the European Parliament in Strasbourg, France," May 8, 1985.

29 Reagan, "Address at Commencement Exercises at Eureka College," Eureka, IL, May 9, 1982.

30 Reagan, "Address to the Cambridge Union Society," Cambridge, England, December 5, 1990, quoted in Frederick J. Ryan Jr., editor, *Ronald Reagan: The Wisdom and Humor of the Great Communicator* (San Francisco: Collins Publishers, 1995).

31 The relationship between Reagan and John Paul II is the focus of my next book. The two men had a warm mutual admiration. They were kindred spirits who shared a worldview (despite one being Protestant and the other Catholic) and were jointly committed to taking down the Soviet empire. Their interests also included domestic issues such as abortion, both of them gravely concerned with what the pontiff called the "Culture of Death." They met several times during and after Reagan's presidency and exchanged numerous letters throughout the presidential period, many of which I have gotten declassified through Freedom of Information Act requests at the Reagan Library. For my previous work on this relationship, see Paul Kengor, *God and Ronald Reagan* (New York: HarperCollins,

2004), pp. 59, 199, 208–225, 276–277, and 283; and Paul Kengor, *The Crusader: Ronald Reagan and the Fall of Communism* (New York: HarperPerennial, 2007), pp. 87–89, 93–98, 113–115, and 133–140.

32 Ronald Reagan, of course, was not Catholic, but he was very close to Pope John Paul II, both personally and ideologically, including in this conception of the relationship between faith and freedom. John Paul II articulated this relationship in his March 1995 encyclical *Evangelium Vitae (Gospel of Life)*, sections 18–20.

33 Joseph Ratzinger, *Christianity and the Crisis of Cultures* (San Francisco: Ignatius Press, 2006).

34 For an extended examination of Reagan's faith, see Kengor, *God and Ronald Reagan.*

35 Reagan, "White House Ceremony in Observance of National Day of Prayer," May 6, 1982. Reagan often invoked this image. Among many other instances, see Reagan, "Proclamation 5017—National Day of Prayer, 1983," January 27, 1983.

36 Reagan, "Weekly Radio Address," December 24, 1983.

37 Reagan, "Weekly Radio Address," May 12, 1984.

38 Reagan, "Remarks at the National Forum on Excellence in Education," Indianapolis, December 8, 1983.

39 In the 1960s, Reagan said this as governor, specifying Jesus as part of the equation: "[T]he answer to each and every problem is to be found in the simple words of Jesus of Nazareth." Among the 1980s examples, see Reagan, "Remarks at the Annual National Prayer Breakfast," February 4, 1982; Reagan, "Remarks at the Annual Convention of the National Religious Broadcasters," January 30, 1984.

40 Reagan, "Remarks at Georgetown University's Bicentennial Convocation," October 1, 1988.

41 Reagan, "Address to the Roundtable National Affairs Briefing," Dallas, TX, August 22, 1980.

42 Reagan, "Address to the Nation on Christmas and the Situation in Poland," December 23, 1981.

43 Kirk stated this in a 1957 booklet titled, *The Intelligent Woman's Guide to Conservatism.* Excerpts were recently reprinted as: Russell Kirk, "Conservatism Requires a Religious Foundation," *Crisis Magazine*, July 22, 2013.

44 See: G. Tracy Mehan, III, "George Will, Unchurched, Defends Religion," *American Spectator*, August 6, 2013.

45 Also a crucial spiritual influence was Reagan's childhood pastor, the Rev. Ben Cleaver.

46 See Ronald Reagan, *An American Life* (New York: Simon & Schuster, 1990), pp. 49, 57, 70, 123.

47 Ronald Reagan, "My Faith," *Modern Screen*, June 1950, pp. 37 and 88.

48 Reagan, Republican convention speech, August 17, 1992. As governor, he wrote a letter to Billy Graham noting his "own optimism based on faith." Letter is quoted in Helene Von Damm, *Sincerely, Ronald Reagan* (New York: Berkley Books, 1980), p. 82.

49 Reagan remarks during the dedication of the Ronald Reagan Presidential Library, California, November 4, 1991.

50 Letter is quoted in Von Damm, *Sincerely, Ronald Reagan*, p. 86.

51 Ibid.

52 See Paul Kengor and Patricia Clark Doerner, *The Judge: William P. Clark, Ronald Reagan's Top Hand* (San Francisco: Ignatius Press, 2007).

53 Ibid, pp. 123–125.

54 The parable has been shared many times, including by speechwriter Peter Robinson at Grove City College during the February 2010 annual Ronald Reagan Lecture.

55 Interview with Richard V. Allen, November 12, 2001.

56 "How Reagan Decides," *Time*, December 13, 1982, p. 12.

57 Reagan, "Remarks to the American Enterprise Institute," December 7, 1988.

58 Of all the Reagan children, none were as close to Ronald Reagan politically and ideologically as Michael Reagan. Michael Reagan is truly his father's son. For a fascinating and moving memoir, see Michael Reagan, *Twice Adopted* (Nashville: Broadman and Holman, 2004).

59 Particularly touching is Patti Davis's book, *Angels Don't Die: My Father's Gift of Faith* (New York: HarperCollins, 1995).

60 Reagan, "Radio Address to the Nation on the American Family," December 3, 1983; Reagan, "Proclamation 5513—National Family Reunion Weekend, 1986," July 29, 1986; Reagan, "Proclamation 5570—National Adoption Week," November 13, 1986; Reagan, "Remarks at a White House Briefing for Supporters of Welfare Reform," February 9, 1987; and Reagan, "Proclamation 5912—National Family Week, 1988," November 19, 1988. When Reagan called the family "the nucleus of civilization," he was quoting Will and Ariel Durant. Reagan, "Radio Address to the Nation on Family Values," December 20, 1986.

61 Reagan, "Radio Address to the Nation on Family Values," December 20, 1986.

62 Reagan, "Proclamation 4999—National Family Week, 1982," November 12, 1982.

63 Reagan, "Proclamation 4882—National Family Week, 1981," November 3, 1981.

64 In a radio address for Father's Day, given June 14, 1986, Reagan stated, "What does fatherhood mean today in America? I guess the same as it always has."

65 In a separate context, for instance, Reagan said, "we've got to teach history based not on what's in fashion but what's important." Reagan, "Farewell Address to the Nation," January 11, 1989.

66 Reagan, "Proclamation 5933—America Loves Its Kids Month, 1989," January 12, 1989.

67 Reagan was tolerant of homosexuals (as Lou Cannon and Reagan's daughter have commented upon at length), but he did not approve of homosexual conduct. In a March 1980 interview with the *Los Angeles Times*, he said that homosexuality represents "an alternative life style which I do not believe society can condone, nor can I." When pressed on his thinking, Reagan said "you could find that in the Bible it says that in the eyes of the Lord, this is an abomination." Source: Robert Scheer, "Reagan Views Issues at Home, Abroad," *Los Angeles Times*, March 6, 1980.

68 At the time of my writing, Ronald Reagan's daughter, Patti Davis, told Politico that she believes her father would not have "stood in the way" of gay marriage if he were alive today. See Kevin Robillard, "Patti Davis Says Reagan Wouldn't Have Opposed Gay Marriage," *Politico*, April 4, 2013. I wrote a response published at CNN.com, titled "Ronald Reagan: Same-Sex Marriage Advocate?" May 1, 2013.

69 Reagan, "Proclamation 5576—National Family Week," November 21, 1986.

70 Reagan, "Radio Address to the Nation on Family Values," December 20, 1986.

71 Reagan, "Proclamation 5576—National Family Week," November 21, 1986; and Reagan, "Executive Order 12606—'The Family,'" September 2, 1987.

72 Reagan, "Executive Order 12606—'The Family,'" September 2, 1987.

73 Reagan, "Proclamation 5912—National Family Week," November 19, 1988.

74 Reagan, "Proclamation 5933—America Loves Its Kids Month, 1989," January 12, 1989.

75 Ibid.

76 Ibid.

77 Reagan, "Remarks at the Annual Conservative Political Action Conference," Washington, DC, February 6, 1977.

78 Ibid.

79 Reagan, "Remarks at the Annual Conservative Political Action Conference," Washington, DC, March 20, 1981.

80 Reagan, "Remarks at the Annual Conservative Political Action Conference," Washington, DC, February 20, 1987.

81 Reagan, "Remarks at the Annual Conservative Political Action Conference," Washington, DC, February 11, 1988.

82 Reagan, "Proclamation 5709—AIDS Awareness and Prevention Month, 1987," September 29, 1987. Also see Reagan, "Proclamation 5892—National AIDS Awareness and Prevention Month, 1988," October 28, 1988.

83 Reagan, "Proclamation 5709—AIDS Awareness and Prevention Month, 1987," September 29, 1987.

84 Reagan, "Remarks on Signing the National Family Week Proclamation," November 12, 1982.

85 Reagan, "Proclamation 5709—AIDS Awareness and Prevention Month, 1987," September 29, 1987.

86 Reagan, "Proclamation 4882—National Family Week," November 3, 1981.

87 There are legitimate questions regarding Reagan's disappointing abortion actions as governor. These were actions that advanced and even legalized abortion in California, and which he came to regret the rest of his career. For an examination, see Paul Kengor, "Reagan's Dark Hour," *National Review*, January 22, 2008. For a particularly touching example of Reagan's private pro-life sentiments as president, see Paul Kengor, "Life Letters," *National Review*, June 30, 2004.

88 Here again, Reagan's thinking was remarkably similar to John Paul II's in *Evangelium Vitae*, which referred to "the right to life" as "the first of the fundamental rights."

89 See William P. Clark, "For Reagan, All Life Was Sacred," *The New York Times*, June 11, 2004. The Fourteenth Amendment (as well as the Fifth Amendment) declares a right to "life," but Reagan would have gone further by supporting and interpreting that right as a right to life for the unborn.

90 Reagan speaking on "Ronald Reagan: A Legacy Remembered," History Channel, 2002.

91 Interview with Bill Clark, July 17, 2003.

92 Reagan, "Remarks to the National Religious Broadcasters Annual Convention," January 30, 1984.

93 The quote is Christ's words. See Matthew 19:14, Mark 10:14, and Luke 18:16.

94 Editorial, "Sermon on the Stump," *The New York Times*, February 3, 1984.

95 Reagan, "State of the Union Address," February 4, 1986.

96 Reagan actually authored and published a book on abortion during his presidency, titled *Abortion and the Conscience of the Nation*, with an afterword from Malcolm Muggeridge (Thomas Nelson Publishers, New York, 1984). It was the only such published work he did as president. Among many references that tie his religious convictions to his pro-life stance, see his "Remarks at Kansas State University," September 9, 1982; "Remarks at the Annual Convention of the National Religious Broadcasters," January 31, 1983; "Remarks at the Annual Convention of the National Religious Broadcasters," January 30, 1984; "Remarks to the Student Congress on Evangelism," July 28, 1988; and "Remarks to the Students and Faculty of Archbishop Carroll and All Saints High Schools," October 17, 1988.

97 Reagan, "Remarks at a White House Briefing for Right to Life Activists," July 30, 1987.

98 See my op-ed on this, "Remembering Roe: A Forgotten Warning from Ronald Reagan," January 24, 2011, posted at the website of the Center for Vision & Values, *www.visionandvalues.org.*

99 Among others, see Paul Kengor, "Obama's Planned Parenthood Love Fest," *American Spectator*, April 29, 2013.

100 See my paper from the April 2011 Center for Vision & Values conference on American exceptionalism: Paul Kengor, "America: 'Shining City . . . Last Best Hope'; An Analysis of Ronald Reagan's 'Time for Choosing' Speech and Farewell Address," Center for Vision & Values, April 2011, posted at *www.visionandvalues.org* and *www.faithandfreedom.com.*

101 Reagan, "America the Beautiful," commencement address, William Woods College, June 1952. Text provided by William Woods University.

102 For a long list of examples, where I cite roughly a dozen incidents between 1968 and 1988, see Paul Kengor, *God and Ronald Reagan* (New York: HarperCollins, 2004). Even then, those citations are far from a complete list.

103 Bill Bennett stated this in his February 2011 appearance at Grove City College for the annual Ronald Reagan Lecture hosted by the Center for Vision & Values.

104 See Kengor, *The Crusader*, pp. 21–27.

105 The best primary source on Reagan's GE tours is an April 1982 oral-history testimony from Earl Dunckel, housed at the Reagan Library and now available on Amazon. Dunckel accompanied Reagan on these visits. The most thorough study of Reagan's GE years is Thomas W. Evans, *The Education of Ronald Reagan: The General Electric Years and the Untold Story of His Conversion to Conservatism* (New York: Columbia University Press, 2008).

106 Reagan, "Inaugural Address," January 20, 1981.

107 Reagan, "Farewell Address," January 11, 1989.

108 Ibid.

109 Ibid.

110 Ibid.

111 Ibid.

112 President Barack Obama, "Remarks by President at Independence Day Celebration," July 4, 2010.

113 In 2010, I did an unpublished study of Reagan's citing of the Founders compared to other recent presidents. I analyzed chief executives going back to John F. Kennedy. I picked six of the most frequently cited Founders: John Adams, Benjamin Franklin, Patrick Henry, Thomas Jefferson, James Madison, and George Washington. I also added Abraham Lincoln. Of course, Lincoln was not present in Philadelphia in 1776, but Lincoln, in so many ways, is a founder, and, more so, a preserver, ensuring and extending those founding principles more than any president and arguably even more than any Founder—as is immediately evident by consulting the Gettysburg Address. Moreover, when our presidents have invoked Lincoln, they have done so in the spirit of the founding and the essence of America and its principles.

My source was the official Public Papers of the Presidents of the United States, also known among presidential scholars as simply the "Presidential Papers," which is the comprehensive collection of every presidential speech, statement, press conference, and interview by a president, published by the Government Printing Office. Those papers are now online for the last few presidents. The government is in the process of putting more of them online. For now, however, most of the papers for presidents back to JFK remain in thick bound volumes; researching them required slower searches in the index of each book.

I also attempted to do tabulations on the number of mentions of the Founders for each president. That data is referenced below, though I urge a crucial caveat: This is not a perfect method. The online search engine, in particular, is alternately off base, but seemingly only to a small degree. Generally speaking, the numbers are good, certainly within an acceptable margin of error. The numbers on George W. Bush and Bill Clinton seemed more sporadic than previous presidents, since information was (presumably) still being compiled.

114 Ronald Reagan with Richard Hubler, *Where's the Rest of Me* (New York: Duell, Sloan & Pearce, 1965), pp. 311–312.

115 An early pre-presidential example of Reagan saying this was his acceptance speech at the Republican National Convention on July 17, 1980.

116 The degree to which Reagan actually succeeded in scaling back the size of government is a big debate that I will not address here.

117 On this, see the excellent works on FDR by Burt Folsom: *New Deal or Raw Deal* and *FDR Goes to War*.

118 Marx and Engels, *The Communist Manifesto* (New York: Penguin Signet Classics, 1998), p. 75.

119 Reagan, *An American Life*, p. 134.

120 Reagan, "Farewell Address."

121 See: Andrew E. Busch, "Ronald Reagan and Economic Policy," in Kengor and Schweizer, eds., *The Reagan Presidency: Assessing the Man and His Legacy* (Lanham, MD: Rowman & Littlefield, 2005).

122 See the Tax Foundation's "History of the Federal Income Tax" at *http://taxfoundation.org/sites/taxfoundation.org/files/docs/fed_rates_history_nominal_1913_2013_0.pdf.*

123 See Busch, "Ronald Reagan and Economic Policy," p. 29.

124 See Busch, "Ronald Reagan and Economic Policy," pp. 29–30; and Matt K. Lewis, "Ronald Reagan Raised Taxes 11 Times? The Real Story," *The Daily Caller*, June 6, 2012.

125 See Hayward quoted in my lengthier analysis (with Mike Reagan): Paul Kengor and Michael Reagan, "What Would Reagan Do About America's Fiscal Crisis?" *FoxNews.com*, December 18, 2012. Also see Paul Kengor, "No Contest: The Reagan Stimulus vs. the Obama One," *USA Today*, August 15, 2011.

126 See Busch, "Ronald Reagan and Economic Policy," p. 36.

127 See Andrew E. Busch, *Ronald Reagan and the Politics of Freedom* (Lanham, MD: Rowman & Littlefield, 2001), pp. 100–102.

128 Ibid.

129 Ibid.

130 See my detailed discussions: Paul Kengor, "Obama's Homeless," *American Spectator*, October 26, 2012; and Paul Kengor, "What About the Homeless? … The Homeless Then and Now—Reagan and Obama," *FoxNews.com*, October 16, 2012.

131 Busch, *Ronald Reagan and the Politics of Freedom*, p. 102.

132 See: "State of Homelessness in America 2012," National Alliance to End Homelessness, posted at *www.endhomelessness.org/library/entry/state-of-homelessness-in-america-2012.*

133 The total U.S. population under Reagan was 236 million, compared to 317 million under Obama. Under Obama, the percentage of the population on food stamps and homeless is likewise much higher than under Reagan.

134 Ibid.

135 Julie Crawshaw, "'Misery' Levels Hit 28-Year High in U.S.," *MoneyNews.com*, June 17, 2011.

136 Reagan, "Inaugural Address," January 20, 1981.

137 Ibid.

138 To view, see *www.federalregister.gov/uploads/2012/03/FR-Pages-published. pdf.* Also see Busch, "Ronald Reagan and Economic Policy," p. 32.

139 See Table 8.4 at *www.whitehouse.gov/omb/budget/Historicals.*

140 See Busch, "Ronald Reagan and Economic Policy," p. 30.

141 See Paul Kengor, "No Contest: The Reagan Stimulus vs. the Obama One."

142 See Office of Management and Budget, "Historical Tables," Table 1.2, posted at *www.whitehouse.gov/omb/budget/Historicals.*

143 Table 1.1, "Summary of Receipts, Outlays, and Surpluses or Deficits, 1789–2018," Office of Management and Budget, Historical Tables, *www.whitehouse.gov/omb/budget/Historicals.*

144 Reagan did cast some blame at the Democratic Congress. In a speech to CPAC in March 1984, Reagan predicted that just as "the critics" were being proven wrong on inflation, interest rates, and the economic recovery, they would one day be wrong on the deficit as well—"if the Congress will get spending under control."

145 Again, to view the data, Google "OMB historical tables" and look at Table 1.1.

146 Reagan, "Speech to Members of Platform Committee," Republican National Convention, July 31, 1968. Speeches filed at Reagan Library, "RWR—Speeches and Articles (1968)," vertical files.

147 Joseph R. Holmes, ed., *The Quotable Ronald Reagan* (San Diego, CA: JRH & Associates, 1975), p. 121.

148 For a handful of 1970s quotes, see James S. Brady, ed., *Ronald Reagan: A Man True to His Word*, (Washington, D.C.: National Federation of Republican Women, 1984) pp. 32–33.

149 "Where Reagan Stands, Interview on the Issues," *U.S. News & World Report*, May 31, 1976, p. 20.

150 Reagan, "First Inaugural Address," January 20, 1981.

151 Reagan, "The President's News Conference," June 16, 1981.

152 Reagan, "Remarks at the Bicentennial Observance of the Battle of Yorktown in Virginia," October 19, 1981.

153 Reagan, "Remarks and a Question-and-Answer Session at a Luncheon Meeting of the St. Louis Regional Commerce and Growth Association in Missouri," February 1, 1983.

154 Reagan, *An American Life*, p. 293.

155 See Paul Lettow, *Ronald Reagan and His Quest to Abolish Nuclear Weapons* (New York: Random House, 2005); and Beth A. Fischer, *The Reagan Reversal* (Columbia, MO: University of Missouri Press, 2000).

156 I have written a chapter on this for an upcoming Harvard University Press volume on Ronald Reagan, coedited by myself and Jeffrey Chidester. To cite just one prominent early example of what I am referring to, consider Reagan's November 18, 1981, National Press Club speech, which first enunciated his "zero-zero option" for taking both sides down to zero levels on INFs (Intermediate Nuclear Forces) deployed in Europe.

157 Reagan, "Remarks to the Conservative Political Action Conference," Washington, DC, March 1, 1975.

158 Located in "Ronald Reagan: Pre-Presidential Papers; Selected Radio Broadcasts, 1975–1979," January 1975 to March 1977, Box 1, RRL. Also see Kiron Skinner, Martin Anderson, and Annelise Anderson, Reagan, *In His Own Hand* (New York: Free Press, 2001), pp. 10–12.

159 The seminal work by Harvard University Press, *The Black Book of Communism*, estimates one hundred million dead due to communism. That book, however, severely underestimates the number of Soviet victims, which, in reality, was likely sixty to seventy million—three times more than the Black Book estimated. For instance, Alexander Yakovlev, in his 2002 work, *A Century*

of Violence in Soviet Russia (Yale University Press), estimated over sixty million dead under Stalin alone. On the influenza numbers, see Gina Kolata, *Flu: The Story of the Great Influenza Pandemic of 1918 and the Search for the Virus That Caused It* (New York: Touchstone, 2001).

160 See, for example, Reagan, "Interview with Reporters from the Los Angeles Times," January 20, 1982; Reagan, "Address at Commencement Exercises at Eureka College," May 9, 1982; Reagan, "Remarks on Signing the Captive Nations Week Proclamation," July 19, 1982; Reagan, "Interview with Morton Kondracke and Richard H. Smith of Newsweek Magazine," March 4, 1985; Reagan, "Interview with Representatives of College Radio Stations," September 9, 1985; Reagan, "Question-and-Answer Session with Students at Fallston High School," Fallston, MD, December 4, 1985.

161 Reagan, "Remarks to the National Association of Evangelicals," March 8, 1983.

162 Reagan, "Address Before a Joint Session of the Irish National Parliament," June 4, 1984.

163 For an extended discussion, see Paul Kengor, "The Communist War on Religion," posted at the website of the Victims of Communism Memorial Foundation, *www.globalmuseumoncommunism.org.*

164 The "opiate of the masses" remark is well known. The source for the quote, "communism begins where atheism begins," is Fulton J. Sheen, *Communism and the Conscience of the West* (Indianapolis and New York: Bobbs-Merrill, 1948). Sheen, who spoke and read several languages, translated the quote into English from an untranslated Marx work.

165 Lenin wrote this in a November 13 or 14, 1913, letter to Maxim Gorky. See James Thrower, *God's Commissar: Marxism-Leninism as the Civil Religion of Soviet Society* (Lewiston, NY: Edwin Mellen Press, 1992), p. 39.

166 For examples, see Kengor, *God and Ronald Reagan*, pp. 249–254.

167 Reagan, *Speaking My Mind* (New York: Simon & Schuster, 1989), pp. 168–169.

168 Ibid.

169 In *Dreams from My Father*, Obama uses the word "collective" eight times in various applications, including "collective history," "collective memory," "collective decline," "collective psyche," "collective redemption," and (among others) "collectively exorcising."

170 Obama said this in a 1995 interview with a Chicago publication. See Hank DeZutter, "What Makes Obama Run?," *Chicago Reader*, December 7, 1995.

171 Reagan owned a 688-acre ranch called Rancho del Cielo in the Santa Ynez Mountains north of Santa Barbara, California. This was a true ranch, where Reagan maintained and rode horses (among other hobbies). Reagan came alive at that ranch, and even insisted that the more he visited the ranch, the longer he would live. During his eight-year presidency, Reagan spent a year's worth of time at the ranch. Today, there is a superb exhibit on Reagan's time at the ranch at the Reagan Ranch Center in Santa Barbara. For details, see *www.yaf.org*. Other testimonies to Reagan as a rancher, horseman, and cowboy include colorful cover stories done in *Classic* magazine (a magazine dedicated to horses and horse riding) in June/July 1977 and in *Cowboys & Country* magazine (Spring 1999), and also the statue of Reagan in his cowboy / ranching gear erected outside the entrance to the Reagan Library, dedicated by the National Cowboy Hall of Fame.

172 See Peter Robinson, "Immigration: What Would Reagan Do?" *Wall Street Journal*, June 15, 2010. Robinson's piece is the best on Reagan and immigration.

173 Ibid.

174 Among other sources, Reagan himself recounts this story in chapter five of his memoirs, *An American Life*.

175 See: Steven F. Hayward, Paul Kengor, Craig Shirley, and Kiron Skinner, "The real story of Reagan and race," *The Washington Post*, September 1, 2013; Lou Cannon, "Reagan's Southern Stumble," *New York Times*, November 18, 2007; Lou Cannon, *President Reagan: The Role of a Lifetime* (NY: Public Affairs, 2000), p. 173; and Anne Edwards, *Early Reagan: The Rise to Power* (NY: Morrow, 1987), p. 53.

176 Reagan, "Remarks at a White House Reception for the National Council of Negro Women," July 28, 1983.

177 Reagan, "Proclamation 5018—Year of the Bible, 1983," February 3, 1983.

178 Reagan, "Remarks at the Annual Conservative Political Action Conference," Washington, DC, February 6, 1977.

179 Reagan, "Remarks at the Annual Convention of the National Association of Evangelicals," Orlando, March 8, 1983.

180 Reagan was here quoting Father Theodore Hesburgh, president of the University of Notre Dame. See: Reagan, "Remarks at the Annual Meeting of the American Bar Association," Atlanta, August 1, 1983.

181 Reagan, "Remarks at a Ceremony Marking the Annual Observation of Captive Nations Week," July 19, 1983.

182 Ibid.

183 Reagan, "Remarks at the Annual Convention of the National Association of Evangelicals," Orlando, March 8, 1983. Also see Reagan, "Remarks at the Annual Convention of the National Religious Broadcasters," January 30, 1984.

184 Reagan, "A Time for Choosing," October 27, 1964.

185 Here, Reagan was referring to Soviet dissident Natan Sharansky, a Jewish dissident jailed in the Gulag for his religious and political convictions.

186 To view online, see: *www.reagan.utexas.edu/archives/speeches/1989/011189i. htm.*

187 I have discussed this with Tony Dolan many times. He refuses to take even partial credit for a speech that he says was "completely Reagan."

188 Draft located in the Ronald Reagan Library, Presidential Handwriting File (PHF), Presidential Speeches (PS), Box 9, Folder 150. Reagan labeled the "young father" page (which he inserted) "14A."

Index